ADVANCE PRAISE

"This book is exactly what most of us need—a credible tool to help us pause and reflect on who we are, where we are going, and what is the impact of our lives. More importantly, it calls us to action and helps us move out in a practical and inspiring way. I'm excited to digest and use it for myself and am already thinking about how I can send a link to share it with so many of my friends and family who can benefit as well. Great book that will change lives, freeing us to attain a higher level of joy and satisfaction."

COLONEL (USAF RETIRED) LEE ELLIS, FORMER POW
1967-1973 NORTH VIETNAM AND ACCLAIMED AUTHOR
OF "LEADING TALENTS, LEADING TEAMS, LEADING
WITH HONOR AND LEADING WITH ACCOUNTABILITY."

"I've had the privilege of working with Greg over the last seven years. His positive impact on my personal and professional life has been profound and greatly appreciated. This book helped me to further understand him and to look deeper into myself in a way that will result in stronger, more genuine relationships. It also reminded me of the importance of taking care of myself, which has often been a 'back-burner item.' Greg, thank you for sharing part of your life journey and for committing yourself to help all of us lead more successful, happier lives."

EW TIBBS, PRESIDENT AND CHIEF EXECUTIVE OFFICER,
CENTRA HEALTH SYSTEM, LYNCHBURG, VA

"I have had the honor of knowing and loving Greg and his family since our service on the West Point faculty. A mentor, role model, colleague, and long-time friend, his style is engag-

ing, welcoming, embracing, and accepting—like pulling up a chair and talking with your best buddy; his message is profoundly insightful, joyful, genuine, and impactful. If you are seeking a richer and fulfilling life that is purposeful, meaningful, honorable, and selfless, then read this with an open heart and mind and you'll be grateful you did—once you start you won't stop!"

MICHAEL MONTELONGO, ACCOMPLISHED BOARD MEMBER AND FORMER CFO OF THE UNITED STATES AIR FORCE

"Greg has worked with me as my executive coach for many years. He has taught me the principles in this book over the years and I can tell you, they work! This book may be as life-changing for you as its principles have been for me. Read it, as Greg writes, "If not for yourself, do it for the people that love you, that count on you and want you to live long and well."

DR. DON KENDRICK, NEUROSURGEON AND CHIEF MEDICAL OFFICER, BAPTIST HEALTH, MONTGOMERY, ALABAMA

"I have known Greg as an exceptional executive coach and masterful leadership educator and his impact upon me personally as well as on hundreds of my organization's leaders has been significant. However, Greg's book gave me an even greater respect and appreciation for Greg's core message and insights regarding the critical importance of creating meaningful habits that sustain our being our very best selves for those we serve, support, love and lead."

LYNN MILLER, EXECUTIVE VICE PRESIDENT OF THE CLINICAL ENTERPRISE OPERATIONS, GEISINGER HEALTH SYSTEM

"*It is my pleasure to recommend this book. Having collaborated with Greg Hiebert for many years, I know him to be a man of the highest integrity and trust. As one reads about Greg's successes, struggles and paths taken, it will help you reflect on your own life, so that you, too, can learn to confidently and courageously take the necessary steps to find personal and professional fulfillment. Imagine what you can contribute if you break the bonds of fear and regret. Greg's book provides the guidance and the emotional support to assist you to live a life worth living.*"

JOEL KOBLENTZ, SENIOR PARTNER, KOBLENZ
GROUP EXECUTIVE SEARCH

"*I strongly endorse this book for not only its immense insights into how to better create a happier and more fulfilling life but for its humanity and insights into what too often gets in the way of living more healthy and productive lives. As a practicing Physician leader, I see too many patients as well as caregivers who make terrible life choices not only about their health but joy and happiness. I have known Greg for many years and his methods and habits are extremely effective and supported by significant evidence and can change us all for the better.*"

DR. KAREN BARR, INTENSIVIST AND ICU MEDICAL DIRECTOR

"*If you are looking for practical tips and perspectives on finding contentment and happiness with who you are and where you are today, look no further than this book! Greg Hiebert offers great advice for finding joy at home and in the workplace. The sooner you read, the faster you can use these tips to increase the happiness in your life!"*

BOB DAVIS, MANAGING DIRECTOR, PIVOT
STRATEGIC MARKETING, INC.

"I've known Greg for almost 30 years in many situations (business school classmate, client, collaborator, advisor and advisee, fellow veteran, and close friend). This book reflects the remarkable person he is. Reading these pages will make your life better. It's made more real by Greg sharing is own struggles in which his helpful words are rooted."

TOM MALLORY, MANAGING DIRECTOR, ACADIA ASSOCIATES

YOU CAN'T GIVE WHAT YOU DON'T HAVE

Creating The Seven Habits
That Make A Remarkable Life

YOU CAN'T
GIVE
WHAT
YOU DON'T
HAVE

GREG HIEBERT

GRAYLINE
PUBLISHING

YOU CAN'T GIVE WHAT YOU DON'T HAVE

Creating the Seven Habits That Make a Remarkable Life

ISBN   978-1-5445-1074-3 *Hardcover*

       978-1-5445-1073-6 *Paperback*

       978-1-5445-1072-9 *Ebook*

This book is dedicated to the loving memory of my older brother, Don ("Dee") Hiebert. He lost his life with the rest of his crew and his Group Commander in a B-52 crash on April 11, 1983, on a training mission. He will always be a beacon for how I should live a remarkable life. He always believed in me, despite having many reasons not to, and not a day goes by that I do not think of him and selfishly wish he was around. He was goodness personified, but he also believed that each day was an opportunity to become better and ensure our lives were as meaningful and rich as possible. I know my family feels the same as I do. I would not be a leadership coach and educator if it were not for my brother's influence, inspiration, and example, and when I am teaching and coaching others, my role model and inspiration is my brother. I am sure Dee would be very proud that this book has been written.

CONTENTS

INTRODUCTION

I was miserable.

I was also successful. I was an executive in a prominent consulting firm and compensated extremely well. I had graduated in the top two percent of my class from West Point, and with summa cum laude honors from Harvard Business School. I had a successful marriage—deeply in love with the gal of my dreams—and three daughters and a son, all healthy and thriving. By all appearances, I was very successful and should have been extremely happy. I wasn't supposed to be miserable, but I was. I lived in a place of frequent moodiness, loneliness, and worthlessness that had consumed me since I was a boy. Now, as an adult, my misery continued. I worked hard all day in a career I was certainly not passionate about. Yet, when I came home, I kept working. I worked to hide my misery from my family.

While I hid my misery well, a dear friend noticed and convinced me to see a pastor at an Episcopalian church who might be helpful. A nagging voice told me that this was something I needed to do for me. I went. I talked to the pastor. He was open. More than that, he was open-hearted, enlightened even.

Yet, he said not even he could help me. He told me I needed the help of a professional therapist.

You didn't go to therapists or even counselors in my family. My father and all of my five siblings had served or were serving in the military. We grew up believing that there was no problem that grit and toughness could not overcome. It was just against the unspoken family rules to seek outside help. You never showed weakness. There was something wrong with you if you did that.

Thankfully, I overcame my reluctance to seek help because deep down inside, I knew that my best thinking obviously had gotten me to where I was. This gentle and thoughtful pastor also recognized that I could use some objective support and compassionately challenged me, "This could be really helpful for you."

After carrying this darkness for so many years, perhaps someone else's thinking might be better than mine.

He gave me a name—Kempton Haynes, the man who would change my life.

I found him on the fifth floor of a nondescript brick building in downtown Atlanta, an annex building of a Presbyterian Church. Despite its downtown setting, Kempton's office felt less cosmopolitan and more like a comfortable living room. Kempton had outfitted it with oversized chairs, oriental carpets, and warm curtains. It was a safe and welcoming place, but what truly made it welcome (and what truly looked the most out of place in downtown Atlanta) was Kempton himself.

Kempton was eighty-two years old and looked like Santa Claus, if Santa Claus had decided to give farming a try. He had snowy white hair and a matching beard that fell onto his denim overalls. From the moment I met him and saw his twinkling eyes, I knew I was in the presence of a good soul. His wide-open smile reached from one ear to the other, and he had a handshake full of warmth and joy. I felt I was in the presence of someone who was unbelievably safe. He was, in a sense, perfect. He never told me what to think. He emitted empathy, compassion, and what I would call grace every time we met. I felt immediately welcome to be my real, most authentic self.

I had never been so uncomfortable.

Kempton sat back and looked at me with his warm, inviting smile, not saying a word.

"I guess I am supposed to talk," I said.

He kept smiling.

"I suppose I am to talk about myself."

And still, he kept smiling.

Finally, it came out.

I couldn't help it. In that space of safe and welcoming silence, I felt this urge to open myself up and share the things I had struggled with for so long. I shared that professionally I had hit a place where I didn't know where to go. I was stuck in this very respectable job that paid well when what I really wanted to do was to teach and help others learn to be more effective leaders. It was my dream, but I couldn't figure out a way to get to it. I had three kids getting ready to go to college, and I didn't know how I would pay for it. My wife, Claudia, a part-time nurse but full-time mom was chauffer to our older children's activities, while also chasing a young toddler, Molly, who was nine and twelve years younger than her siblings. A career change seemed out of the question and would be incredibly disruptive to our lives. It was probably the darkest period of my professional life.

I told him more. I told him that, beyond my career, I lived with tremendous insecurity, with voices that said I wasn't enough.

He kept smiling.

I kept talking.

I told him when I was five or six that I thought I overheard my mother tell my father in a burst of anger, "You know we had him by mistake," referring to me. My little brain must have concluded that I was a mistake. I told Kempton about the teacher I'd had in first grade who had touched me—and, I would later learn, others—in sexual and destructive ways. I told him about the bladder reflux condition I'd had as a boy that caused me to urinate in my clothes and that my father frequently thought it was just an issue of my inability to control myself. I recall too vividly when I was six that my father punished me for soiling my clothes by putting a diaper on me and even now writing this, I still feel great shame. I was just six, but it certainly intensified my feelings of worthlessness.

I'd been carrying all that around with me for so long it had become normal. It became so normal that, later, when Kempton told me to take a self-improvement course that required writing a personal paper, the title came easily: "Greg, the Unlovable, Worthless Failure."

That was the deep wound I'd been carrying around since my early childhood. I was afraid that if you really knew me, if you stripped away all the masks and façade, you'd see Greg, the true Greg, the imposter, the unlovable and worthless failure.

The defining, transformative moment came in our fourth session. It was one of the rare moments Kempton spoke, perhaps the first time he shared what he really thought. Finally, I was about to hear some kind of wisdom that might prove helpful.

I listened.

"Man," he said. "I'd hate to be your wife."

It took a moment for it to sink in, and for me to reply, "What? Why?"

"Because it's clear to me that you've put so much of your joy in life and your happiness on her shoulders and certainly not yours," he said. "It's clear she's one of your only friends. She's your lover. She's your wife. And it must be hard being her."

It hit me like a ton of bricks.

When I asked my wife, she confirmed, too enthusiastically,

what I already knew: Kempton was right. She said it was tiring for her to not only have to carry the heavy burden of dealing with headstrong teenagers and a toddler but also trying to keep me happy. She felt that I resented her going to her book club and maintaining a strong social circle, as I did not have much of a social circle myself beyond her and just a few very close friends who I did not spend much time with.

Sometimes the truth hurts. But when we confront that truth head-on and realize that our current way of living is not working well, that truth can give us the fire and courage to actually do something about it. Kempton's courage to speak this truth became my catalyst for starting down this path to take responsibility for my life. After that conversation with Kempton, I felt a shift inside me. I knew it wasn't my wife's job or anyone else's to make me happy.

It was my job.

It was my job to overcome the idea that I was an unlovable, worthless failure. It was my job to learn that those feelings didn't negate the things I loved and was proud of: my success at West Point, the accolades from Harvard, all the talents I'd been given and gifts along the way, including my marriage. It was my job to realize that if my wife saw me as I saw myself that, after eighteen years of marriage, she wasn't leaving me. She'd still love me. And my kids, despite all of my shortcomings, would still think I'm a great dad. It was my job to confront my own demons and say to myself, "You don't need to keep carrying these."

It was time for a change.

I continued to meet with Kempton one-on-one. I also began attending group sessions he led for people dealing with similar issues. He thought the group would be a way to gain perspective and social support.

I did gain perspective. What I found was that the people in the group had tremendous emotional pain, and while they felt great safety in being able to vent and share their pain, what intrigued me was that many in the group had been there for a number of years and they seemed to share past traumas of broken relationships and unhappy lives as if it had been only yesterday. One participant continually referred to his ex-partner as "the bitch" with immense anger, and I was shocked when I heard that he had been divorced for over five years. While it was a safe place for us all to talk, I wasn't seeing a lot of healing, and I knew that I wanted something different for my life. At the time, I couldn't name what I was looking for, but words like peace, joy, happiness, grace, and freedom seemed much healthier pursuits than anger, cynicism, bitterness, and frustration.

In my self-improvement course where I wrote my paper,

"Greg, the Unlovable, Worthless Failure," I learned a lot about storytelling. I learned that we can't change the facts, but the story, and how we interpret those facts, is up to us. I left that course knowing I had the freedom to create a new story that was much more empowering than my existing story, something that my fellow group members were struggling to learn.

I hoped they would learn it, but I knew that environment, a place where the stories never changed and were only being retold, was no longer the place for me. I realized that I had been a member of that group of storytellers for a long time, long before I had even met Kempton.

When I was in eighth grade, I read a short but powerful book by Richard Bach, *Jonathan Livingston Seagull*. That book spoke to me about how we give up much of our freedom to fit in and conform to what society indicates is the safe and more predictable path. To this day, there is a quote from the book that stays in the recesses of my mind: One of the seagulls, who broke free of the flock and became a teacher of acrobatics and revolutionary flight, says to one of his students who has crashed into a stone wall, "Maynard Gull, you have the freedom to be yourself, your true self, here and now, and nothing can stand in your way. It is the law of the great gull, the law that is."

For so many years, I wanted to claim that power, but

Chapter 1

WELL-BEING

ROBERT

Robert was a young administrator in a large hospital. Still in his mid-thirties, he was already being groomed to replace the hospital's CEO. He had married his high school sweetheart and had a beautiful family. He was also courageous—courageous enough to tell me, once we met, that he did not expect to live long.

He wasn't sick, but he wasn't healthy, either. He was working—always, always working. Even when he went to bed, his phone and iPad were on his nightstand while he slept (and when he didn't sleep). He would take calls at any hour about anything happening at the hospital. Throughout the night, he would roll over, grab his iPad, and check how the hospital was staffed against patient demand.

He was scared. He feared failure; he was scared that something would go wrong and that as the number two person in command of all hospital operations, something could go wrong, and it would be his fault.

He was also scared for his family. He knew his lifestyle was unsustainable but didn't know how to change. He was afraid that it would eventually kill him and that he would leave his wife and young children alone, while also not fulfilling his full potential.

But he didn't know how to live, how to work, any other way. Extremely driven, he had found success early in life when he started a highly successful software company as a teenager. Years down the road, Robert's father, a very successful (but at times controlling) businessman, wanted Robert to inherit the family business. Like me, Robert realized that those deep wounds from childhood—for Robert it was his own feelings of not being enough that drove him toward overcompensating through drive and achievement—don't just go away. In fact, they can follow us and influence us into adulthood. Robert was working hard for the hospital and for his family, but it was also his way of saying, "No, I'm not going to take a thing from my father. I'm going to prove to him that I can do this all by myself."

Robert is one of the sharpest executives I have worked

with and he was wise enough to know that as he stepped up into an even more senior leadership role, he needed to be a more positive role model that included leading a more balanced life, as well as exercising greater emotional maturity. The outgoing CEO was wise and knew that Robert could benefit from the support of an executive coach. I felt privileged to get the call.

When I begin working with a client, I often start with a "360 leadership assessment" that gathers anonymous input from all the people who work with and around the client regarding their perceptions of the client's leadership strengths and opportunities for improvement. My belief is that what you think of your own leadership effectiveness is insignificant in comparison to those who experience it, and I find that often, leaders have major blind spots to how they show up and interact with others. Over the course of the last 16 years, I have personally given leadership feedback to well over 1,700 leaders, and it is always a meaningful and humbling experience for me to help another human being understand their impact, positive or negative, on others.

In Robert's case, there were major concerns about his level of anxiety—and the tremendous levels of anxiety that caused among the rest of the staff. People can be very careful in these surveys if they think that their feedback may not be completely anonymous. However, in this case they were courageous enough to give their "unvarnished truth" in the 360 and it turned out to be a great wakeup call for Robert.

To Robert's credit, he was very self-aware. He knew he was in a dark place and he knew he could benefit from a journey to what he called emotional maturity and better well-being. He worried about how he treated people. He knew at times that he wasn't good at managing his own emotions. He knew that the work he put so much into was in danger because of how much he neglected his personal life—sleep, exercise, vacations, his relationships with his family.

"I'm not sure I'll live till I'm forty," he would often joke with me.

But he was willing to start. He just needed to know where.

One of the first things Robert learned was that, while he felt his purpose was to serve others, he had to incorporate living long and well into that purpose.

It wasn't easy, but to his great credit, he did not wade slowly into making significant changes regarding his physical, emotional, mental, and even spiritual well-being. He jumped into exercise with great gusto. He put his iPad and smart phone away from his night stand. He openly shared his commitments with his wife, who was equally ecstatic with his well-being commitments. He worked hard to be less reactive at work and was careful to guard his words as well as his body language when his team members said things he would have once ridiculed or judged.

In short, he started to focus on the primary thing he'd been neglecting all along: himself.

Once he did that, his work—the thing he was finally learning to distance himself from—began to improve.

Where he'd once dismissed leaders that worked for him when they were not as quick to grasp new ideas or to seize initiative the way he would, he now reminded himself to give them attention and respect and even restraint before he responded. The team that surrounds him is now much more positive, creating a better work environment for everyone. He lost weight. His wife is more appreciative of him, and his kids see him more often.

None of this was easy at the start. It was a matter of cultivating a life and creating habits. And once those habits were created, things began to change.

Robert and the previous CEO passed the baton of leadership even sooner than planned and the transition was incredibly positive and successful. Robert is in his new role as CEO, and the board couldn't be more pleased.

Robert is happy, too, but not just about the job. I saw him recently, after he'd taken his family on vacation, where he'd made only one phone call to the hospital. He's more confident and comfortable sharing responsibility with his team. He spent five days on the beach with his wife and kids.

And that iPad? He didn't look at it once.

Sometimes, we must let go to fully claim our lives back.

WELL-BEING

What Robert learned was to be aware of the importance of his own well-being.

But what is well-being?

I define it as being healthy and fit.

Those aren't the same things.

Healthiness and fitness are two distinct concepts. Think, for a moment, about a very healthy person who is unfit; they're not taking any medications; their cholesterol is normal; their weight is within normal guidelines. They don't have any diseases, and during their annual checkup, their doctor gives them a clean bill of health. But if they were to run a sprint, they'd be winded after fifty meters. They couldn't run a half mile if you paid them. Healthy, sure. Fit? Nope.

On the flipside, think about a marathon runner, someone who exercises so much that they can eat whatever they want, and they do. Then they chase those foods with a cigarette. Fit? Absolutely. Healthy? Not even close.

You need both—and not just of the body, but of the mind and spirit also.

A book I return to over and over is Viktor Frankl's *Man's Search for Meaning,* which chronicles the author's struggle as a prisoner in a Nazi death camp in Auschwitz. Few books from the last century have had greater impact on helping change people's lives than this one. When Frankl returned from the concentration camps to Vienna, his home before being imprisoned by the Nazis, he realized he had lost everything. His mother had been gassed, his brother killed in another camp, and his wife starved to death in Bergen-Bergen. He wondered, what was the point in going on with life? He turned to writing and in an empty room with bombed-out windows, he wrote *Man's Search for Meaning* in just nine days. Two of the most powerful things he wrote were: "*Everything can be taken from a man but one thing: the last of the human freedoms—to choose one's attitude in any given set of circumstances, to choose one's own way,"* and, *"Between stimulus and response there is a space. In that space is our power to choose our response. In our response lies our growth and our freedom."*

These two quotes lie at the foundation of this book and probably thousands of other books dedicated to helping people take greater responsibility for their joy, happiness, and well-being. I think about these two quotes at least weekly, and sometimes daily, as I reflect that even in the horrors of a concentration camp where your captors could take everything from you, they could not take what was in your head and they could not take away your capacity to choose your attitude and response.

I had spent a good portion of my life believing that so much of my attitude was out of my control and so I remind myself as often as I can that I can always choose my own way. And the second quote reminds me that I will have greater capacity to choose my own way if I am thoughtful about my response and am much more intentional regarding the life that I want to choose and create.

Through our mind-body-spirit connection, the more we are intentional about cultivating ourselves in terms of our physical, emotional, and mental well-being, the more capacity we have to see that space, and the more capacity we have to choose our best response.

If Frankl can do that in the face of such great difficulties, any of us can.

In fact, some difficulty can even be necessary.

THE IMPORTANCE OF STRESS

A common error in the search for well-being is the avoidance of stress.

One of the early pioneers in studying stress, Hans Selye, was one of the first to study an interesting phenomenon: without some moderate level of stress, human beings don't perform well. There's an optimal level of stress, but it changes for each of us based upon our capacity to endure stress.

Take, for example, Olympic swimmer Michael Phelps. To win twenty-seven gold medals, Phelps is much more in tune and comfortable with incredible levels of stress. In fact, it continues to bring out the best in him. It's similar with the members of a Navy SEAL team. They're trained to endure intense levels of stress because when they're going into a mission, that's what they're going to have to face. So, while we do need to inoculate ourselves against the hazards of stress, we also can raise our threshold to how much stress we can take and how well we can perform with that stress.

We hear a lot these days about soldiers returning home with post-traumatic stress disorder (PTSD), but we don't always get the full story. Sadly, about 10 to 15 percent of soldiers and Marines coming back from combat in Afghanistan or Iraq suffer from chronic PTSD. In the last ten years, however, we're finally beginning to use some different language: post-traumatic growth. Post-traumatic growth (PTG) is defined as positive psychological changes in one's outlook, disposition, and even belief system experienced as a result of the struggle with a major life crisis or a traumatic event. The idea that human beings can be changed by their encounters with life's challenges, sometimes in radically positive ways, is not new as the idea is present in spiritual and religious traditions, literature, and philosophy. However, what is new is that psychologists, counselors, and scholars are systematically studying the concept and using their research and insights to help others accelerate growth in response to difficult, challenging circumstances.

As researchers are studying the phenomena of PTG, they are seeing that an even larger portion of returning soldiers and Marines come back psychologically stronger and more capable and can transfer that strength to their everyday lives.

What's the difference between those soldiers and Marines whose experiences lead them to chronic post-traumatic stress disorder and those who experience post-traumatic growth?

Broadly speaking, it's their thinking. It's the way we choose to see and remember things. Victor Frankl showed us how in his book, *Man's Search for Meaning*. Could you even imagine facing what Frankl did when he was released from Auschwitz? The horrors he saw are unimaginable and then when released, to find out that most of his family and friends did not survive. How does one pick up the pieces from such trauma? He did by pouring himself into a new purpose in his life. His famous concept of Logotherapy is based on the idea that the greatest motivation for human beings is a "will to meaning" and an inner pull to find a significant purpose and meaning in life.

I love the story he shares in an interview:

> "*Once, an elderly general practitioner consulted me because of his severe depression. He could not overcome the loss of his wife, who had died two years before and whom he had loved above all else. Now, how could I help him? What should I tell him? I refrained from telling him anything but instead confronted him with a question, 'What would have happened, Doctor, if you had died first, and your wife would have had to survive you?' 'Oh,' he said, 'for her this would have been terrible; how she would have suffered!' Whereupon I replied, 'You see, Doctor,*

*such a suffering has been spared her, and it is you who
have spared her this suffering; but now, you have to pay
for it by surviving and mourning her.' He said no word
but shook my hand and calmly left the office."*

There is a huge difference between the person who comes
back from trauma broken and depressed and hurt, and
the person who sees the trauma and creates a story about
how it has made him or her even stronger, more capable,
more appreciative of life, and more determined to make
their lives even more meaningful.

It's about how we choose to see it. Please don't misunderstand me. This is not simple or easy and in no way am
I making light of anyone who has suffered or is suffering
from PTSD. It is a terrible thing. Just in the time I've been
writing this book, we have watched in horror the mass
killings in Las Vegas, New York City, a small town outside
of San Antonio, Texas, and most recently in Parkland,
Florida. I cannot even fathom how those who were there
and lost loved ones might get their lives back to normal.
What I am saying, though, is that going through trauma
does not doom a person to depression and unhappiness.
We can use the trauma as Frankl did, to define more intentionally our purpose in life and to live that purpose with
greater determination, joy, and happiness.

My first-grade teacher was an abuser. And while she

abused many others besides me, her abuse seemed to fit the narrative of my life that I held on to for far too long of Greg the unlovable, worthless failure. But through my own journey and seeing that I could change my story, I chose a much more empowering one. I don't see myself as a survivor now. And one of the ways that I have grown through my own trauma is to help human beings (beginning with myself) be more compassionate and supportive to and with one another.

I have experienced sadness and even some anger through the years that this teacher could do what she did to such vulnerable and innocent children. Yet, I have learned that to hold on to resentment and anger only hurts me. Buddha said it well: "When we hold on to our anger, it is like poisoning ourselves but expecting the other person to die." My primary emotion these days is resignation that humanity still treats humanity so terribly and to make sure that I am not a contributor to that suffering and that I am doing my part to be a healer. I'm not avoiding the stress of my past trauma; but instead I'm acknowledging it and using it to be a better human being. There are unspeakable horrors in this world. In fact, I remind myself of them daily. But rather than be discouraged by all of that, I have made the choice to be a promoter of something good and positive.

My youngest daughter, Molly, is a perfect example of

someone who has used difficulty and challenge to be a stronger, more determined person. When Molly was thirteen, our oldest daughter Emily warned us that Molly was so thin that she was unhealthy. Emily can be blunt, so her actual comment was, "She looks like a Somali refugee." (I apologize to anyone from Somalia.) Her comment catalyzed the decision by my wife, Claudia, and I to take action and seek help at the Atlanta Center for Eating Disorders.

To Molly's credit, she realized and accepted that she had an eating disorder. Diagnosed with anorexia, Molly took on her disease with great courage. Only a year or so later, she was diagnosed with narcolepsy. This disease is one that the medical profession still knows so little about, and the treatment is only focused on managing the symptoms instead of curing the disease. As a young adult in her last year at George Washington University, Molly will assure us that having narcolepsy puts a significant cramp in your social life. And still, I have never heard Molly complain or rail at the unfairness of life. Instead, I have watched with great pride as she uses her battle with anorexia and narcolepsy to grow stronger and more capable. Her view is, "Look, I have narcolepsy. I don't know why I got it. Science has no idea how to heal it. All they can do is treat the symptoms, and I refuse to be defined by my narcolepsy. I just have to manage it."

She's remarkable. She's an inspiration.

This is one of the most important themes of this book. What we need to live remarkable lives is within all of us, but it begins with this openness to reflect and say, "Where can I be a better human being? Where can I be a better parent, leader, spouse, and sibling and what do I have to change in me?" It begins with a commitment to take better care of yourself, so you have the energy, thoughtfulness, and intention to have the very best life possible.

THE SCIENCE OF WELL-BEING

In the mid-1980s, Martin Seligman was appointed as president of the American Psychological Association. He had an insight: we have studied brokenness and abnormal psychology ad nauseam. Then, it struck him: if we started studying the people who embody well-being and happiness, couldn't we learn a tremendous amount from them rather than continuing to study broken people?

He wasn't criticizing the studies that had been the basis of modern psychology, but he was saying it was time to pay attention to the happy people, the optimists, the people who, no matter how difficult the circumstances around them, are positive and optimistic and joyful.

He wanted to know: What are they doing?

He figured it out.

It's important, before we get into the specifics, to take a moment to recognize just what an extraordinary shift it was to go from studying sick and unhappy people to studying happy and mentally healthy people. That shift became a revolution. This is significant: our whole notion of happiness changed from seeing happiness as something to aspire to, to seeing happiness as the precursor to having a remarkable and successful life.

If we want happiness in our own lives, so, too, must we change our notion of what it is.

Seligman went on to identify the different factors in the lives of mentally healthy people. He came up with an acronym, PERMA, to remind us of the five critical factors: Positive emotions, Engagement, Relationships, Meaning, and Achievement. He describes these in great detail in his book, *Flourish*, and here's a brief description of each of these:

Positive emotions are one of the key tools used by the military in helping returning soldiers from the battlefield readjust to normal life back home. They teach them the concept of "hunting for the good" as a way to operationalize soldiers cultivating more positive emotions in their lives. These lessons include practice opportunities, such as role-playing with teachers who take on the role of a soldier's spouse and attempt to engage in meaningful dialogue. This allows the soldier to practice distinguishing positive versus less than positive responses to their spouse. "Hunting for the good" is about shifting our attention from seeing what's wrong and not working, to deliberately seeing what's right and working well. We will devote significant parts of the chapter on positive emotions toward improving our ability to hunt for the good.

I use that expression in much of my client work. In fact, I often begin my work, before diving into any material, before getting into any specific issues and problems, by asking the simple question: what are the bright spots going on right now for you in your professional and personal life? There's tremendous research that says when we are in a place of *positive emotion*, we're more creative. We see greater possibilities. We're more optimistic and certainly more innovative. And that positivity, like so much else, can be cultivated.

Engagement is actively and enthusiastically participating in the activities of our lives that help us grow, learn, and give us joy. A few nights ago, Claudia and I, along with our dear friends Sarah and Peter, attended "The Adult Prom" at a famous Atlanta Science Museum where we danced for several hours to the music of a great band. From what we could tell, we were much, much older than the other participants and we had a blast. If you were to see the pure joy on our faces, that might give you a sense of what engagement looks like.

Everyone is different and we all find enjoyment in different things, whether it's playing a sport or an instrument, singing, dancing, practicing yoga or meditating, working on an interesting project at work, or a hobby. *Engagement* is when these activities completely absorb our attention, creating a 'flow' of joyous immersion into the activity. And when we are in this state of flow and *engagement*, it stretches our social, emotional, and intellectual intelligence.

Human beings are meant to be social and communal. We need *relationships*. We are meant to live in and belong to tribes, and yet so many of us choose to be isolated, creating all sorts of problems with our mental, physical, and emotional well-being. Technology hasn't made things any better. We might think we're connected through a computer screen, but real relationships are personal and meaningful and allow us to be our best selves.

To flourish, to borrow Seligman's word, one must also have a sense of *meaning*. It's the same thing Frankl observed and chronicled in his book. Frankl realized as an observer in Auschwitz, that people who had hope for their lives also had a sense of meaning. They had purpose even within a Nazi death camp. When you have something worthwhile to live for, it allows you to not only survive but thrive, even during difficulty and challenge. One of the central themes of well-being is that you're living life with intention, that there is meaning to choose and meaning to pursue. Meaning is a powerful motivator, perhaps one of the greatest there is.

Finally, Seligman believes we must also have *achievement in our lives*. Not only do we need to have significant meaning, but we need to be moving and striving toward a sense of goal and outcome accomplishment. It's essential to have hope and optimism that in this journey, we're moving toward even better things, and achievement provides us with tangible evidence of that progress and accomplishment.

In a delightful book, *The Progress Principle*, authors Teresa Amabile and Steven Kramer explain how seemingly mundane workday events can make or break employees' inner work lives. But it's *forward momentum* in meaningful work that creates the best inner work lives. Through rigorous analysis of nearly 12,000 diary entries provided by 238 employees in 7 companies over the course of 5 years, the authors explain how leaders can foster progress and job engagement every day by providing clear goals and autonomy, as well as giving employees meaningful feedback on their progress to include sincere comments of appreciation, recognition, and encouragement.

Seligman's five elements of flourish: Positive emotion, Engagement, Relationships, Meaning, and Achievement, are powerful enablers of a life well lived. I hope to show later in this book how to make these elements a habitual part of one's life.

OPTIMISM

Seligman wrote another meaningful book, *Learned Optimism*. Optimism often gets a bad rap and, perhaps, not for bad reasons. Many people get selected for positions of leadership and responsibility because they're good at seeing the problems and fixing them. They're very good, in other words, at seeing what's wrong.

This is a necessary component to organizational and communal life. We need problem solvers. We need skeptics. We need the pessimists from time to time to help us not be complacent with the status quo. But too much pessimism and too much criticism destroys relationships. Pessimists aren't always the happiest people to be around.

There's a quote I like to use that is said to come from the Jewish Talmud: "You don't see the world as it is. You see the world as you are." I believe that's true. If everything I think about as a spouse or a boss or as a parent is negative, if all the people I care about only hear what's wrong with them and what's wrong with the world, it's not the basis for a substantive, loving, caring relationship.

Approximately a year ago, I spoke to a group of about

sixty radiologists about what they could do to build lives of greater joy and happiness through intentional self-care. At the end of the talk, one of the radiologists came back to talk to me. He said matter-of-factly, "Your habits for happiness are nothing but a life hack to man's condition." I said (after a slight pause so I could move emotionally from being slightly defensive to being curious), "What do you mean?" He explained that we're genetically disposed toward anxiety, because it's a survival tool and it is deeply wired into our genetic makeup. He's right. The caveman optimist who saw the tall grass moving and just thought it was pretty, probably didn't survive very long.

The good news today is that rarely do we have to be so anxious and fearful around every corner. Of course, we shouldn't stop being thoughtful and careful in certain circumstances, but most of us don't have to live in a constantly anxious state.

Because of the speed today by which bad news moves, it is quite easy staying in our highly anxious state. However, the research is also abundantly clear that when we are highly anxious over long periods of time, the impact on our lives can be lethal. Not living in that anxious state, however, can take some work.

Consider a young soldier or Marine who's been in combat and has been carefully trained to be hypervigilant in battle.

He or she had to be hunting for the bad because that's how you stayed alive. Think now about how detrimental that is when that young soldier or Marine goes back to their young family and their two-year-old drops a glass. If that soldier is still living out of that primal state, it can lead to some harsh reactions. So, we must learn instead to hunt for the good to complement our natural disposition toward hunting for the bad. As we train ourselves to see the good, we realize it is all around us. It's a simple tool that becomes an important part of everyday life, with many applications.

It's not rocket science, either—just ask Seligman. In the introduction to *Learned Optimism*, he talks about getting after his eight-year-old for biting his nails. His son replied, "Well, Dad, I'll stop biting my nails if you will stop being such a grouch." It caused Seligman to think, "My gosh, here I am, one the foremost psychologists and teachers, and I haven't used any of this to make me a happier person."

That was, of course, until he decided to.

WELL-BEING'S IMPORTANCE TO SOCIETY

Each of us comes into the world with different capabilities and talents, and it's been my experience that if every human being could better cultivate those strengths, they'd be more productive. They'd be happier, and more fulfilled. This book is about helping others be, ironic as it may sound, a bit more selfish. By cultivating self-care, everyone can be better at serving and taking care of others.

Now, I want to be clear, this book is not about creating a self-indulgent mindset focused on me, myself, and I. At the heart of my habits for leading a remarkable life is indeed to make our lives substantially more for ourselves so that we can help and serve others in more extraordinary ways. At the heart of this book is that we must be in service to others, but when we don't have the energy, enthusiasm, and excitement within us, it is darn near impossible to have it for others.

Robert, my client at the beginning of this chapter, is a prime example of that. Robert is providing much more positive, impactful leadership to those around him because of his own self-care.

He's far from the only one. I can remember working for bosses who didn't like to take vacations and who didn't like you taking yours either. They were often the ones who made sure that no matter how long they stayed at work, you had to stay until they had left, regardless of how late it was or what family responsibilities you had. That kind of environment isn't very satisfying, and it makes it hard to focus on yourself.

But when you are taking good care of yourself, you can be your best—and not just for yourself but for others. And in turn, society gains from that positive contribution. It is a fact of life that our interactions with others impact them, and they us. Therefore, why not try to make those interactions as positive and meaningful as possible? Why not be the kind of person that others enjoy working with? There continues to be growing research that the most successful teams, marriages, and relationships have the highest ratio of positive interactions to negative. We will explore this more, but I want to plant an important seed: when we are at our best, we help others to be at their best as well.

We all influence everyone around us. Much of it is subconscious. When I am in the presence of a healthy, optimistic person, it's hard for that not to positively influence me. Google spent millions of dollars on a study called Project Aristotle to study teams around the globe. They wanted to know the attributes and characteristics of the best teams and who the best team leaders were. Sure enough, the best leaders were the most positive. They were the ones who made it safe for every person on the team to speak out and feel valued and respected. They were the most supportive and encouraging, constantly giving of themselves to their team members so the team members could be their best selves. It is a wonderful, virtuous cycle.

If we look at those leaders, we will find that they are much healthier, and their well-being is tended to. They're in a place where they're able to pay attention to someone on their team who may not be contributing as much as they used to. They notice when teammates harshly criticize others and (privately) tell them they're not contributing to the positive nature of their team's ability to get its work done well.

Our own well-being, in other words, allows us to not only influence each other positively, it allows us to look out for one another.

Amid great despair and suffering, Viktor Frankl wrote about watching one prisoner take a small piece of bread and break part of it and give it to another prisoner who, perhaps, was suffering from hunger even more. He saw prisoners being deliberately supportive and compassionate to their fellow prisoners in an environment where you'd think each person would look out only for themselves. What Frankl teaches us is that when we cultivate this intentional well-being in ourselves, it manifests in serving the rest of humanity.

THE ROADBLOCKS TO WELL-BEING

I was once so defined by my insecurities, so defined by this childhood psychological wound of not being enough, that I let that define what my journey would be. I thought

I could only be happy and deserve to be happy when I had gotten to a destination where all my insecurities were gone. I longed for a time when I would be enough. I would have enough money, a big enough title or promotion, or be smart enough, or accomplished enough that I could then be truly happy. I had defined myself by these goals, and I didn't deserve to be happy until I achieved them.

Many of us make this mistake. In the best seller *Happier: Learn the Secrets to Daily Joy and Lasting Fulfillment*, Professor Tal Ben-Shahar, who teaches one of the most popular courses at Harvard University, describes one of the dominant archetypes of happiness decision-making as that of the "rat racer," who lives for future gain by sacrificing the present. In his book, he writes: "Attaining lasting happiness requires that we enjoy the journey on our way toward a destination we deem valuable. Happiness is not about making it to the peak of the mountain nor is it about climbing aimlessly around the mountain; happiness is the experience of climbing toward the peak."

How often do we hear people say, "Man, wouldn't my life be set if I were to win the lottery?" The reality is that regardless of whether you win the lottery or not, whatever you bring with you into that follows you. Just because you now have a few hundred million dollars in the bank, does that suddenly eliminate all the insecurities or all the ways you've been treating people? Does it transform you?

Of course not.

(I know what you are thinking. "Of course, I would be different if I won the lottery! I will be one of the rare ones who truly will use my fortune to make my life incredible." However, there has been significant research done on lottery winners and, regrettably, despite having greater financial wealth, the long-term happiness and joy for many winners actually decreases.)

The lottery is an oft-used example, but it's a good one. It's an easy fantasy because it allows us to win without having to work for it. It's not that none of us wants to work. In fact, most of us have goals and desires we yearn to strive for.

And yet we don't.

Why? Because we convince ourselves that our goals are unworthy.

Our brains are wired this way. But they don't have to be.

There was once a belief that the brain was hard-wired by the time we were around seven or eight years old. Many neuroscientists believed that by age eight you might learn more, but that you were only filling your fully developed brain with more stuff. They believed that our neural pathways were fixed and that our brains grew no more neurons.

In the 1960s, Richard Davidson, a professor at the University of Wisconsin, proved that wrong by studying a group of Tibetan monks. He demonstrated that they could, through deep meditation, show unique brainwaves. They were showing how the neural pathways were actually growing well into adulthood. Neuroscientists call this concept neuroplasticity, the ability of the brain to modify its connections or re-wire itself, and Davidson's discovery with the monks gave it new life.

The Buddhists say that meditation is a way to manage the "monkey mind," or our propensity to wander off and be easily distracted. But they also say that attachments are what get human beings into trouble. One of the four noble truths of Buddhism is that to be human means that you will suffer, and that we all die, but also that so much of human suffering is created by our crazy thinking. That suffering is created by attachments—attachments to the idea that you or someone else shouldn't be a certain way, attachments to wanting or thinking you need more money, attachments to the conviction that life is unfair. I think of my attachments to the ideas that until I had become and achieved enough, I wasn't allowed to be fully happy or joyful and think about how much pain and suffering I inflicted on myself for so many years. (And probably inflicted on many others.)

Therefore, to avoid so much self-inflicted suffering, we

must develop new ways of thinking. That's hard work. And when something is hard, we often give up, even if—sometimes especially if—we know our goal isn't the final destination but a point along a journey, and that our goals and desires are worthy of our time and hard work.

Because sometimes hard work is, well, hard. It can be discouraging. Sometimes there's not a lot of joy and therefore one of the most important ways for us to hardwire new ways of thinking is in creating stronger habits that guide us toward better ways of being and living.

As I wrote this paragraph, I was reminded that I rode twenty miles on my bike this morning. Bike riding has become a habit that not only gives me great joy but is keeping me healthier. At mile seventeen, I'm not sure I felt any joy. There are days when I don't want to get up and ride my bike. There are days when I don't want to engage in mindfulness. Yet, these habits have become part of who I am and what I do to keep me at my best. And so, I work through whatever mental or physical barriers are in the way because I know that, when I practice the habits, my life really works.

To do that, there's something else I need to cultivate: resilience.

Chapter 2

RESILIENCE

Approximately six years ago, I had been asked by a health system's board to coach the organization's Chief Executive Officer who had been in his role for close to a year. While the CEO perceived himself as a brilliant, transformational, and charismatic leader, the board had received significant feedback, especially from its medical staff, who perceived him as arrogant, lacking in interpersonal skills and integrity, and quite divisive.

I had coached the previous Chief Executive Officer, who was deeply respected and revered for successfully leading the health system for well over thirty years, and through that relationship I had come to know the senior executives in the organization reasonably well. This included the Chief Operating Officer, who I will call Edward. Edward was deeply respected by his colleagues for his strong and compassionate leadership. The previous CEO had mentored him well and strongly advocated that Edward be a candidate as his replacement. Regrettably, the firm handling the CEO search felt that their external candidates were much stronger, and the board acquiesced to their influence. In fairness to the board, the man they eventually hired did present himself well as a brilliant healthcare strategist with a reputation for successfully turning around two previous healthcare organizations. As I engaged this new CEO in a coaching relationship and conducted significant interviews with his key stakeholders, I began to have concerns about what I was hearing regarding his erratic and self-centered behavior.

In time, the CEO began to be very critical of Edward. While he could not find fault with Edward's results and his effectively managed departments, he would voice concerns about Edward's character and the perceived lack of senior executive capabilities. Very possibly, the CEO knew that Edward had been an internal candidate for the role and was widely respected across the organization and community, and therefore felt threatened by Edward's strong relationships even among board members. The CEO would heavily scrutinize the things Edward was responsible for and try to find fault at every turn. He even went as far as trying to get other organizational leaders and physicians to turn against Edward, while at the same time telling Edward that he would mentor him so that he could one day be a great candidate for Chief Executive Officer, presumably at a different healthcare organization.

As I continued to interview people in the organization, I learned more about how the CEO worked but also more about Edward. When Edward and I first connected, he told me how difficult the situation was and that it was abundantly clear to him that the CEO was trying to paint a very negative picture of him in order to eventually fire him or force him to leave the organization. I began to see how the CEO would distort the truth to his benefit, emphasizing certain things to make him look better and diminish Edward's accomplishments. The CEO's strategy was to be perceived as the savior on the white horse, fixing all the organization's shortcomings. The CEO often targeted Edward and other subordinate leaders to make a case that the organization had been a disaster before he arrived. This wasn't true, of course, but I came to discover that this was the CEO's modus operandi.

It also became clear to the CEO that trying to find fault with Edward was not an effective strategy. Perhaps it had worked elsewhere but not with Edward. Instead of taking it personally, Edward showed an incredible sense of confidence that threw the CEO for a loop. Where some people would go into survival mode, Edward just got better. He became clearer on how to lead, how to stay calm, and how to carry out his responsibilities. Rather than get angry,

Edward saw this as an opportunity to grow and to be clear and purposeful about what he had responsibility for and what was at stake for the organization.

I will never forget a dinner that I had with Edward at a local restaurant. Edward's mother had to drive him to the restaurant because, unknown to anybody in the organization, Edward had a significant health challenge that required a surgical outpatient procedure. As Edward was still in great pain, he couldn't even drive himself yet, and he did not trust the CEO with the information about his health challenges as he thought the CEO would use this against him. Despite being in great pain, Edward was determined to give the organization his very best because he deeply cared about the people he served and until the CEO fired him, he would work wholeheartedly to help the organization, despite the upheaval that the new CEO was creating.

I also found working with this CEO to be quite challenging, as I could not get him to take any responsibility for his shortcomings in how he treated others or his erratic behavior. I began to have doubts about his success at his previous "turnarounds" and was finally able to get several executives that had previous experience with him to provide more accurate insights into what Edward, I, and many in the organization were experiencing.

Unsurprisingly, these executives shared that their experiences were quite similar, and that this CEO had been highly disruptive and divisive. After hearing those perspectives, I shared my serious reservations with the board in a formal report, stating that I couldn't in good conscience continue the coaching engagement and that if this CEO were to continue in his role, the CEO's impact on the organization would be significantly harmful. As my first paragraph to the board stated: "*Throughout my thirty-two years of work experience in the military and civilian worlds, I have not taken on an assignment that presented as much personal internal conflict and challenge, and for that reason, this final report is extremely difficult to write.*"

Fortunately, a week later, the CEO resigned, and the board immediately promoted Edward into the CEO position where he has been leading the organization successfully ever since.

My belief is that it wasn't just Edward's performance as Chief Operating Officer that had impressed the board. It was their great respect and recognition of his ability to continue to perform well even under extremely stressful circumstances.

In other words, they were impressed by his resilience.

At West Point, I had learned that a key element of successful battlefield leadership was the ability to show tremendous grace under pressure. Years later when I was helping the Army gain even more insight into the characteristics of highly effective small unit combat leaders, I conducted dozens of interviews with young soldiers regarding what they thought the most trusted and respected leaders did to gain their confidence and I heard a phrase frequently in those interviews: "Sir, when the $%#& hit the fan, my leader was calm and confident!" This quality of being able to stand in the storm without becoming part of the storm certainly is an important quality of leadership that Edward was able to demonstrate to his board and organization, and I continue to see as one of the most important qualities for having and sustaining a remarkable life.

So, let's dig more deeply into this wonderful quality of resilience.

WHAT IS RESILIENCE?

We hear about resilience in terms of people all the time, but I like the way it's defined by chemists. In chemistry, resilience is the capacity of a substance to recover and return to its original form, shape, and quality, even after significant changes. A piece of rubber, for example, is very resilient. It can get squeezed by a vice, but when the vice is removed, the rubber goes back to its original shape.

We can apply the chemist's definition of resiliency to humans, too. Recently, a prominent physician leader I coach was telling me about telomeres. Telomeres are the caps at the end of each strand of DNA that protect our chromosomes, like the plastic tips at the ends of shoelaces. Without the coating, shoelaces become frayed until they can no longer do their job. It is the same with telomeres. As telomeres wear down, DNA strands become damaged and our cells can't do their job. Therefore, the length of our telomeres (they look like little hairs) have a significant impact on how long we live. Comprehensive research tells us that prolonged stress significantly shortens our telomeres and certainly plays a significant part in affecting the quality and the length of our lives. This means that resilience is important beyond the workplace since this capacity to bounce back, recover, and inoculate ourselves against future stress is a key to a long and well-lived life.

If this all sounds easier said than done, that's because it is. But it can be done. Resilience doesn't show up overnight. A key theme of this book is that for anything important to show up in our lives, we must cultivate it, practice it, and make it an integral habit so it can be sustained against the many distractions and demands of life.

THE RESULTS OF RESILIENCE

Edward was able to help other employees move on from

the negative CEO by so positively modelling his own capacity to not let the negativity and significant challenge of the previous CEO's leadership define him. Instead, he used this time to refine his character and develop even greater leadership qualities.

Because of the deep bonds he formed across the organization, his resilience was contagious. It's possible those around him didn't realize what resilience they were showing themselves. With Edward's positivity leading the charge, the rest of the organization mirrored that attitude and the organization has truly thrived and prospered under his resilient, positive leadership.

In the book, *The Power of Full Engagement*, authors James E. Loehr and Tony Schwartz provide a set of ideas and tools to help their readers function at optimal levels of performance. At the heart of their wisdom is the fact that: "Energy, not time, is the fundamental currency of high performance." As part of that wisdom, Loehr and Schwartz believe that to be fully engaged with life, we must follow these four key principles:

- Principle 1: Full engagement requires drawing on four separate but related sources of energy: physical, emotional, mental, and spiritual. These sources are what Loehr and Schwartz refer to as the "Pyramid of Full Engagement."

- Principle 2: Because energy diminishes both with overuse and with underuse, we must balance energy expenditure with intermittent energy renewal.
- Principle 3: To build capacity, we must push beyond our normal limits, training in the same systematic way that elite athletes do.
- Principle 4: Positive energy rituals—highly specific routines for managing energy—are the key to full engagement and sustained high performance.

In the physical domain, well-being is a three-legged stool of good sleep, good movement, and good nutrition. If you've got those three things, you've got a solid foundation for the next level of the pyramid, which is emotional connectedness—something essential for someone like Edward, with so many others who relied upon him and who he relied on as well. The more aware you are of your emotions and the emotions of others, the better your relationships will be. And, as we've seen above, the deeper your relationships are with others, the more resilience you're likely to show.

Without knowing it, Edward incorporated the principles from the Pyramid of Full Engagement into his life at a time when he was facing great challenge and difficulty. He was having terrible back problems, so it was hard for him to exercise, but he was mindful of that and again did the resilient thing and maintained frequent physical therapy.

He stayed very grounded to his emotional well-being by staying connected to his colleagues and community; he stayed very focused and mentally clear; and he stayed true to the principles of integrity, service, compassion, and character in the pursuit of a purpose bigger than his own self-interest, shaping his spiritual alignment.

THE OBSTACLES TO RESILIENCE

I'll say it again: cultivating resilience in the face of difficulty isn't easy. We are programmed to focus on the negative aspects in our life, to look for and find the bad, and it's easy to believe what we so often tell ourselves: that things won't, or can't, get better. Seeing the positive can be especially hard in today's world, when we're constantly bombarded through the media with negative stories, images, and videos. Even if each individual story is true, it can, over time, seriously distort our view of reality.

The 24/7 news cycle with the additional bombardment from Twitter, Facebook, and other social media certainly makes it seem like things are worse than ever, but the real facts tell another story. For example, in 1972, there were over 1,000 bombings in the United States and the amount of discord across the country as evidenced by the number of protests was deep and wide. If you ask the average person who was alive back then if they remember 1,000 bombings, they'll say no. The difference between then and now is the media. In 1972, we did not have a ubiquitous press that when a story gets picked up it gets told on every news channel for the next twenty-four hours. Today, for example, if there was a shark attack in South Florida caught on camera, it would not be unusual for the media to show that image over and over again. As humans, we are highly disposed to anything that's a threat to our survival. Seeing the image of a shark attack played constantly feeds the human perspective that we should be afraid of going to the beach. In reality, only a handful of people in the world die each year from shark attacks.

In America, well over 100 people die each year from dropping their hair dryers in a sink or bathtub filled with water. In the United States in 2016, it was reported that more than 300 people died from falling off ladders and hundreds die from allergic reactions from bee or wasp stings. But the media doesn't show us those dangers. They are not newsworthy, and consequently, we don't see the world accurately but as filtered by so many others to include our own filters. And if there is a foundational element to being resilient, it is in realizing that our view of reality is distorted and filtered by our limited experiences as well as shaped and distorted by what we are exposed to.

Because we are bombarded by the most significant bad things happening in the world, it is easier to be more anxious about the state of our lives. And yet, the quality of our lives for most of us, especially in America, has never been higher, as we have much safer transportation modes, much safer homes, much greater capacity to manage the temperature and environment of those homes, better access to nutritional food, and certainly healthcare advances that have greatly lowered death from heart attacks, chronic diseases, infections, and other ailments that were life threatening in the 1950s and '60s. What is sad is that despite the immense progress we have made in so many areas affecting our lives, our satisfaction as a society has actually declined. Other facts supporting this point:

- Depression rates today are 10 times higher than in 1960.
- Fifty years ago, the average age of depression was 29.5; today it is exactly half of that-14.5.
- 94 people die each day from drug overdoses; 121 people die of suicide.
- 75 percent of Americans in 1940 reported being "very satisfied"; today that number has dropped to below 70 percent.

A big part of cultivating resilience is being aware of how our thinking and filters shape the world we see. When we recognize this, we have the capacity to think and choose to see the world differently. When we do that, we can clear the path toward a more resilient, happier lifestyle.

Let's take a look at a few of those obstacles.

THE MYTH OF WILLPOWER

Willpower is not enough to maintain resiliency. As we've seen above, resilience isn't a matter of digging your heels in, as we often tend to think of it. It's the ability to grow, adapt, and keep going in a positive direction even when the direction we're going has to change. In fact, especially then. One of the quotes I often reflect on regarding resilience: "We can't always expect the storms to not come; instead we must learn to dance in the rain." It says that to be human means that literal and figurative storms will come into our lives and if you want to have a remarkable life, you must equip yourself physically, emotionally, mentally, and spiritually to maintain your best self despite whatever calamities and challenges come your way. Certainly, intention is an important element of building resilience, but it must also be accompanied by disciplined habits and actions that can be maintained even when you are exhausted and worn out.

Think about weight loss. If willpower was so, well, powerful, very few would be obese. And yet, we have an obesity epidemic in America that has shown growth year after year since the late 1960s. Fewer and fewer people are setting New Year's resolutions because they know they mostly fail. Most diets, for example, are built simply on the person having enough willpower to stick to the diet and yet when the person stops the diet, they most often go back to the same weight at which they started the diet. More effective diet programs like Nutrisystem are far more successful because they don't rely solely on the dieter's willpower. You get your shipment of carefully prepared foods and you eat what they ship to you. As long as you do that, you're going to get fewer and more nutritious calories. What we often think of as a motivation problem is really an exhaustion problem. Additionally, we often fail to see what we are up against regarding the bombardment on TV for delicious, but high-caloric food, as well as the enticements from other media sources. Imagine yourself in a deep state of hunger, going into your refrigerator at 2 a.m., knowing that there is a container of Häagen-Dazs Rocky Road just calling your name. Not many of us have the willpower to resist that! For far too many of us, we willpower ourselves to an early death.

LOW SELF-ESTEEM

Low self-esteem is another common obstacle to cultivating resilience. Psychologists tell us that most of us experience some kind of psychological wound early in our lives and families of origin. As I've mentioned, my psychological wound was thinking I overheard my mother say I was a mistake. Couple that with my struggle when I was young of making it to the bathroom without wetting my pants and not knowing that there was a medical cause for that and how I saw myself as abnormal, and certainly undeserving of love. And, the more I've opened myself up to share my early psychological wounds, the more other people have opened up with me about their own deep insecurities.

This may sound a bit arrogant but the more that I have shared my insecurities with others, the less power and significance these insecurities seem to have over my life. Yet, I also know that far too many human beings use whatever trauma and difficulty they experienced in their lives as reasons why they cannot have the lives they dream of. Ernest Hemingway wrote these words in his magnificent book, *A Farewell to Arms*, that I reflect on and share frequently, "The world breaks everyone and afterward many are strong at the broken places." Why do some grow while others don't in the broken places? Lucky? Born on the right side of the tracks? Got all the breaks? My belief is that a good portion of the answer lies in seeing our ability to reframe our experiences and choose new attitudes and actions based on that reframe.

As I have written previously, the Buddhists teach in their core Noble Truths that because we are mortal, we will all experience pain, loss, and suffering. And so much of human suffering is rooted in our attachments, our thinking, and our inability to accept the impermanence of all things. We get attached to our childhood traumas and insecurities as the reasons our lives are so insignificant or meaningless. Our thinking that if only the world would make life easier for us, we would find happiness or success. Marianne Williamson in her book, *A Return to Love,* challenges us to not let our insecurities and internal voices say, "I am not enough." Here is an excerpt:

> *"Our deepest fear is not that we are inadequate. Our deepest fear is that we are powerful beyond measure. It is our light, not our darkness, that most frightens us. Your playing small does not serve the world. There is nothing enlightened about shrinking so that other people won't feel insecure around you. We are all meant to shine, as children do. We were born to make manifest the glory of God that is within us."*

DREAMING SMALL

Beyond the obstacles of low self-esteem, there is a notion that our dreams are too outrageous or as Marianne writes above, that we're not worthy enough of them.

Why do we convince ourselves that we're not worthy of our dreams?

It's the ego protection mechanism. To ensure our egos don't get damaged, we never set our dreams big in the first place, or our subconscious tells us we're not capable of achieving the dream. If we don't try to realize the dream, there's no failure. Ego protection then says it's someone else's fault—lousy parenting, grew up without enough opportunities, not smart enough, not good-looking enough, etc.

OVERCOMING THE OBSTACLES

While my journey with Edward continues as he is now the CEO of his health system, I often think about his strength of character that I was able to observe, seeing him effectively manage himself in dealing with a toxic boss. I would like to think that I was able to play a small part in supporting Edward by affirming his strength of character and his resilience and by asking him, "What are you doing to make sure you are your best each and every day?"

Look at that question. I asked *Edward* what *he* was doing to make *himself* his best every single day.

I gave a talk at my church last year titled, "It's Not Your Job to Make Me Happy." I quoted heavily from Viktor Frankl's *Man's Search for Meaning*, and how he survived concentration camps by finding personal meaning in the experience, which gave him the will to live through it. He went on to later establish a new school of existential therapy called logotherapy, based in the premise that man's underlying motivator in life is a "will to meaning," even in the most difficult of circumstances. I have reflected on the following quote thousands of times as it continues to challenge, inform, and transform how I view life and, hopefully, how I live life:

> *Everything can be taken from a man but one thing: the last of the human freedoms—to choose one's attitude in any given set of circumstances, to choose one's own way.*

If Frankl can choose his attitude and find meaning in a hellhole like Auschwitz or Dachau, certainly I can choose purpose and an attitude in my life, which is much richer and safer than a concentration camp.

The famous American psychologist Gordon Allport wrote these words in the preface to Frankl's book:

> *"As a long-time prisoner in bestial concentration camps, Viktor Frankl found himself stripped to naked existence. His father, mother, brother, and his wife died in camps or were sent to gas ovens, so that, excepting for his sister, his entire family perished in these camps. How could he— every possession lost, every value destroyed, suffering from hunger, cold and brutality, hourly expecting extermination—how could he find life worth preserving?"*

Even in the degradation and abject misery of a concentration camp, Frankl could exercise the most important freedom of all—the freedom to determine one's own attitude and spiritual well-being. No sadistic Nazi SS guard could take that away from him or control the inner-life of Frankl's soul. One of the ways he found the strength to fight to stay alive and not lose hope was to think of his wife. Frankl clearly saw that it was those who had nothing to live for who died quickest in the concentration camp. The following lines from the book give clarity as to how each one of us can choose to reframe our experiences, as terrible as they are, in order to help us regain and maintain our resiliency. These words are so profound and powerful that they need to be shared:

We stumbled on in the darkness, over big stones and through large puddles, along the one road running through the camp. The accompanying guards kept shouting at us and driving us with the butts of their rifles. Anyone with very sore feet supported himself on his neighbor's arm. Hardly a word was spoken; the icy wind did not encourage talk.

Hiding his hand behind his upturned collar, the man marching next to me whispered suddenly: "If our wives could see us now! I do hope they are better off in their camps and don't know what is happening to us." That brought thoughts of my own wife to mind. And as we

*stumbled on for miles, slipping on icy spots, supporting
each other time and again, dragging one another on and
upward, nothing was said, but we both knew: each of
us was thinking of his wife. Occasionally I looked at the
sky, where the stars were fading and the pink light of the
morning was beginning to spread behind a dark bank of
clouds. But my mind clung to my wife's image, imagining
it with an uncanny acuteness. I heard her answering me,
saw her smile, her frank and encouraging look. Real or
not, her look then was more luminous than the sun which
was beginning to rise.*

*A thought transfixed me: for the first time in my life I
saw the truth as it is set into song by so many poets, pro-
claimed as the final wisdom by so many thinkers. The
truth—that love is the ultimate and the highest goal to
which man can aspire. Then I grasped the meaning of the
greatest secret that human poetry and human thought
and belief have to impart: The salvation of man is through
love and in love. I understood how a man who has nothing left in this world may still know bliss, be it only for a
brief moment, in the contemplation of his beloved. In a
position of utter desolation, when a man cannot express
himself in positive action, when his only achievement may
consist in enduring his sufferings in the right way—an
honorable way—in such a position man can, through
loving contemplation of the image he carries of his beloved,
achieve fulfillment.*

In front of me, a man stumbled and those following him fell on top of him. The guard rushed over and used his whip on them all. Thus, my thoughts were interrupted for a few minutes. But soon my soul found its way back from the prisoner's existence to another world, and I resumed talk with my loved one: I asked her questions, and she answered; she questioned me in return, and I answered as my mind still clung to the image of my wife.

A thought crossed my mind: I didn't even know if she were still alive, and I had no means of finding out (during all my prison life there was no outgoing or incoming mail); but at that moment it ceased to matter. There was no need to know; nothing could touch the strength of my love, and the thoughts of my beloved. Had I known then that my wife was dead, I think that I still would have given myself, undisturbed by that knowledge, to the contemplation of that image, and that my mental conversation with her would have been just as vivid and just as satisfying. "Set me like a seal upon thy heart, love is as strong as death."

Can you imagine the incredible mental and emotional resilience of Frankl to reflect on the great love he shared with his wife, and the power of his imagination to be inspired by that love, even while being marched to some God-forsaken work camp?

For anyone, regardless of where they find themselves,

taking control of their own thoughts and lives is not always easy. Some of us, like Edward, have resilience instilled in us early in childhood. His resilience also came from his upbringing. Edward is from a small town in the South that suffered one of the highest per capita losses of life in World War II. He learned grit and gratitude from his parents, who were farmers. His father was loving, yet tough and demanding. He taught Edward to never give up. Others have resilience instilled in us through certain transformative experiences that become touchstones for us later in life.

In the summer of 1979, at the age of nineteen, I had the privilege of being selected by my West Point Tactical Officer to attend the US Army Ranger School with fifty-nine other cadets. This school continues to be a physically and mentally demanding experience that truly tests your grit and resilience in extraordinary ways. Out of the more than 200 soldiers and cadets that started the course, we graduated with half of that and surprisingly I was selected by the Ranger Cadre as the Class Distinguished Honor Graduate. My older brother was an Air Force Captain and B-52 Pilot stationed at Warner Robbins Air Force Base in Georgia and I was never prouder than when he drove to Ft. Benning, Georgia, and at the graduation, pinned my coveted Ranger Tab on my shoulder. And when I start to doubt my abilities and my insecurity, I think of that young nineteen-year-old graduating and earning his Ranger Tab and I regain my footing and confidence.

We haven't all been to Ranger School, but many of us do have something that can remind us of our own potential and resilience. Sometimes when I am coaching clients that are facing difficult challenges in their personal or professional lives, I have them take inventory of all of the resources they have at their disposal. Resources such as their faith, friends, family, education, experiences, accomplishments, and difficulties that they have overcome, and they and I are always amazed at just how much they can draw from those things that become lost in the fog of their difficulty.

In addition to our resources, the research is mounting that resilience can be taught, learned, and cultivated in very deliberate ways.

ENERGY MANAGEMENT

In the book mentioned earlier, *The Power of Full Engagement*, the authors talk about being incredibly deliberate in managing our energy. We're all given the same amount of time—twenty-four hours a day, seven days a week. We can't create more time, but we can create more energy. Energy to be used to be at our best for those we lead, support, serve, and care about. This concept of energy management comes from the world of sports and high performing athletes—Michael Phelps and Roger Federer, for example—who are masters at managing their energy, training at the right time, and recovering at the right time, so that when they need to be at their best, they can deliver. Their work can apply to the rest of us, too. Energy is the currency of human connection. It is the critical currency to me being able to teach well, coach well, communicate well. So, the more energy I have, the more I'm able to marshal all of my resources at the right time and place so that I'm truly at my best.

I had never thought of it that way before: if I was disciplined and intentional about how I used and conserved my energy, I could be more energetic and actually use my time much more wisely. This idea hit home for me. For most of my adult life, I had deprived myself of sleep. It started as a cadet at West Point where I held on to this Neanderthal concept that strong people did not need as much sleep and that with effort and focus, one could learn how to live life fully with less and less sleep. (Clearly, the research has put this craziness to bed, no pun intended!) Each Sunday night, I would start my plunge into getting less and less sleep each night. It was no wonder I was completely exhausted by the end of each day. At the end of the work week on Friday afternoon, I wanted nothing more than to crawl up into a little ball and sleep. At a time when I should have been fully present with my family, I was at my lowest energy. When you're at your lowest energy, it's impossible to be your best, or to be resilient despite one's willpower or motivation.

We'll visit this in more depth in a later chapter.

STRENGTH IN COMMUNITY

Sebastian Junger has written about how the strength we find in ourselves is fueled by those we surround ourselves with. He was a war correspondent for years and wrote a book called *Tribe: On Homecoming and Belonging*. In it, he makes a weighty case that perhaps some of the prolonged post-traumatic stress disorder that veterans experience after serving in Iraq or Afghanistan has less to do with the trauma they faced on the battlefield and more from the loss of the deep and intimate human bonds they formed with their comrades in combat. Many a vet will speak about the irony of having to go to war to find the greatest peak experiences of their lives. Resilience isn't just a matter of toughing it out solo. As a country, we haven't done enough to help veterans find new ways to create those bonds that became, for many of them, the closest bonds they've ever had with other human beings.

I often speak about this internal battle many Americans face between their need for autonomy and independence and their need to belong and fit in. On one hand, the great mythology of America is the reflection of the rugged individual—picture John Wayne or Teddy Roosevelt—who are able through the strength of their character, grit, and determination to overcome great adversity and save the day. However, what is most true is that life is a team sport and that little to nothing of significance in the world was created by any one person. The research continues to show us that isolation is incredibly unhealthy and leads to higher rates of depression, burnout, and suicide. The healthiest people in the world are those who feel a great sense of belonging and connection with others.

One of Edward's greatest strengths was his ability to build deep bonds with his colleagues and other key stakeholders in his life. Some of Edward's detractors point to his strong loyalty to others as potentially clouding his objectivity. I have come to see his strong loyalty to others as not only a great strength but also a means to help him and others be more resilient and able to undergo the trials of difficulty and adversity with greater ease. Edward cultivated a deep sense of connection to community in and across his organization, and this gave him a foundation of resilience to draw upon and even deepen, as he has successfully led his organization through turbulent waters.

DWELL ON THE POSITIVE

To make this point again, we're hardwired to focus on the negative aspects in our life and in everything around us. We can combat that by dwelling on the positive. It may feel like that's easier said than done, but we can all do it. It begins with the recognition that there is a fundamental difference between being positive and negative. Once you've done that, ask yourself if you believe you will be happier and more successful by being more positive. Many believe they're successful because they are better than anyone else at seeing the negative. When you are more positive, though, you see less of life as a threat and more of life as an opportunity. That allows you to solve more complex problems because your mind is more open. Your mind is open because you're not fearful and protective. And over time as we have better trained ourselves to see the positive, even when we encounter the negative, our capacity to bounce back and regain our resilience quickens and strengthens.

SMILE

No, really, just smile. Go ahead.

The research around the simple process of smiling is compelling. If you're feeling negative, fool yourself. Smile. A person who has loomed large in my life is John Bonviaggio. He lives on Staten Island and I met him well over twenty-five years ago when as a faculty member at West Point, I was helping lead religious retreats for cadets. John's history is quite unique. He openly shares that he never got past fifth grade and his first profession was a sanitation worker in Manhattan. Over time as John hauled people's trash, he found his calling in ministering to (in his words) "the drunks and the forlorn of the Bowery." Whether it was to clothe, feed, or befriend, John found that while many had discarded those he found on the street much like the garbage he collected, he was committed to giving these men and women their dignity. As he would often say, "God doesn't make junk." Because John's life became one deeply rooted in service, I found him to be one of the happiest and most joyful people I have ever encountered. And while I have had the privilege to meet extraordinary people with immense wealth, education, fame, and accomplishment, I don't think I have ever met anyone as wise and loving as John Bonviaggio. One of his favorite sayings is, "If you're happy, notify your face," and as I write this, I wish you could see the great smile on my face reflecting on this giant of a human being.

As medical technology allows us to better see into the workings of the human brain, we know now that when we smile, chemicals are transmitted in our brains that make us happy and more content. When we frown, sneer, or feel angry, chemicals are transmitted that make us more negative. We have come to know that these negative chemicals are consistent with the fight or flight response, so we become protective, careful, and distant.

GET PERSPECTIVE

Each morning, I use a simple framework called "The 6 P's

for Profound and Positive Living." It is a tool that helps me have clarity and focus for my day (we'll get more into the framework later in the book). Of the six P's, the fifth P is perspective. It is a powerful tool that continues to help me maintain my resiliency. One of the ways I use perspective is to dwell upon a picture that I keep in my notebook. This picture is of a seven-year-old girl holding a two-year-old in their village in northern Nigeria. It was taken four and a half years ago, on the same day Boko Haram, an ISIS affiliate, went into the girls' village, killed the men and took the women for wives and slaves. They also cut off the hands of some of the children. As I have a two-and-a-half-year-old granddaughter, Estelle, seeing the little girl in the picture with a bandage on a stump at the end of her little arm always conjures immense sadness and compassion.

Why would I punish myself every day by bringing up these emotions? I look at this picture to remind me of the craziness of the world we live in, that human beings could inflict such pain and horror on the lives of innocent children, and all that these two precious little girls did was to be in the wrong place at the wrong time. It gives me immediate perspective.

When I want to complain about not getting an extra towel in my hotel room or my plane gets delayed or the internet went down or whatever insignificant inconvenience happens in my life, I remember this story. Thinking about the terrible things the two girls in this picture have had to endure opens me up to gratitude. I live in a country where these things thankfully seldom occur. My family is not threatened or killed because of my religion. I live in a country that is safe and orderly. We have laws to protect us and the majority of us follow these laws. I connect with the negative image of what happened to those girls and then I contrast my own life. It reminds me to not feel sorry for myself and to do something meaningful with my life because I've been given so much and so much has come to me by just being in the right place at the right time. You have to be positive because there's so much in your life to be positive about.

RIDE THE ELEPHANT

When I teach change leadership to clients, I often borrow a metaphor from Jonathan Haidt, a sociology professor at New York University's Stern School of Business. He simplifies our understanding of the complex brain by describing the two parts of the brain—the brilliant thinking brain (the prefrontal cortex) and the emotional brain. The two parts of our brain are always working together, but they work differently. The emotional brain is like a big, lumbering elephant and the thinking brain is like a little man sitting on top of the elephant, trying to get it not only to go but to go the right way. This metaphor is powerful because it provides us with an easy way to differentiate how our thinking can be so strongly influenced by our emotions and vice versa, and it is this interchange that helps us engage, or resist and block change.

We forget that if I asked you to run to the store to buy a jar of jelly and you had no experience with jelly, you might be easily overwhelmed with the choices. At most large chain grocery stores, there are probably forty-five different kinds of jelly on the shelves. If I asked you to analyze the different kinds of jelly before choosing one, you wouldn't get very far, as our thinking brain, the prefrontal cortex, is amazing at analyzing complex things, but it tires very quickly and is easily overwhelmed when the number of things it has to analyze gets beyond a handful. Too often when we think people are unmotivated or confused, it's often just that their brain is tired and overwhelmed by all the things it is being asked to analyze and comprehend. Heck, as I am getting close to sixty, I struggle to even remember a seven-digit telephone number just seconds after someone has told me the number!

Drawing upon the elephant-rider metaphor, if you don't get the elephant going, the rider can be there all day but the elephant is going nowhere. Or if the elephant goes off in the wrong direction, the rider's got to figure out how to steer him back on course. That puts people in a fight-or-flight scenario. A person's prefrontal cortex completely shuts off when they are in a fight-or-flight response. The prefrontal cortex wants to take time to do it right, but in fight-or-flight, we have to respond instantly, so there's little blood going to the prefrontal cortex; instead, blood is moving to our arms, hands, legs, and feet so we have the energy to respond to the threat. When we think about the rider on the elephant, we should remember that he's often exhausted and overwhelmed. When we want people or organizations to change, we have to figure out strategies that will help the rider stay focused and only try to manage a few things. Then, we have to motivate the elephant by appealing to their emotion. Often the adage of 'winning hearts and minds' is about figuring out how to direct the thinking brain and motivate the feeling brain in parallel.

And sometimes, the very best thing we can do for people who are trying to manage very complex and demanding lives is help shape the path so that they can use their limited thinking power in much more focused ways. We can make change easier for people.

Throughout this book, we will speak to the power of habit as a means to shape the path for people to make better choices. Going back to our discussion on trying to lose weight, let's look at how we can shape our paths: the best thing we can do for ourselves is to eliminate anything from our kitchens and cupboards that is not good for us; make sure we shop when we are not hungry; get smaller plates and smaller utensils; get to-go boxes at the start of a meal at a restaurant and put half the usually oversized portions into the box, while not letting the server bring us bread; never go to an "all you can eat" buffet and, if we do, don't sit close to the buffet line. All of these are key strategies to employ so that you are not completely dependent upon your limited brainpower and willpower to make the best choices for you.

ADVERSITY'S SILVER LINING

There is a silver lining to adversity. As I wrote previously regarding Hemingway's quote: "The world breaks everyone and afterward many are strong at the broken places," it reminds us that resilience is not just something that we either have or don't have; it can be taught, learned, and cultivated.

In Chapter 1, we explored the incredible work of Dr. Martin Seligman on positive psychology. His work on resiliency has been just as groundbreaking and impacting. Several years ago, he was able to convince the United States Army that training leaders and equipping them to teach their soldiers about resiliency before and after deployments to Afghanistan and Iraq could have a significant impact on the health and well-being of the Army, to include the reduction of depression and suicide.

Seligman's resiliency skill is quite consistent with the

quote from Victor Frankl that continues to challenge and transform me:

> "*Between stimulus and response there is a space. In that space is our power to choose our response. In our response lies our growth and our freedom.*"

One of the key foundational elements that Seligman brought to the Army was that resiliency could "be built through a set of core competencies that enable mental toughness, optimal performance, strong leadership, and goal achievement." The competencies that were component parts of resilience were: 1) Self-awareness; 2) Self-regulation; 3) Optimism; 4) Mental Agility; 5) Strengths of Character; and 6) Connections. Additionally, he helped the US Army dispel many of the myths surrounding resiliency. Let's take a look at a few of these myths.

Resilience is *not* about:

- Suppressing emotions; it's about regulating/expressing them appropriately.
- Individuals in isolation; it's about relying on yourself and relying on others.
- Handling everything on your own; asking for help is a resilient strategy.
- Acting quickly in every situation; sometimes slowing down is necessary.

- Big accomplishments; it's also about bouncing back from challenges.
- Always being composed or graceful; sometimes it's muddling through.
- You either have it or you don't; it can be taught, learned and developed.
- There is a final destination that, once you have reached it, you are done; instead, it's a continuous process that you can work on and continue to cultivate and develop.

Dr. Seligman built a core resiliency skill in his program for the Army around this very concept of seeing the space and responding to the space with thoughtful and intentional action. Seligman's resiliency skill is called the ATC model where A stands for Activating Event (or stimulus), T stands for our Thoughts (or space) and C stands for the Consequences of those thoughts.

Essentially, Seligman's model calls for us to thoughtfully pause before responding and even to think about the most optimal outcomes for you and the situation you are in. For example, if your spouse criticizes you, before you respond with an equally harsh remark, pause and ask, "What do I want in my relationship with my wife? What does she want in her relationship with me?" Let your answers to those questions guide your response. I suggest clients take a couple of deep breaths and smile when they are responding to potentially difficult comments.

Whether it is a conversation with your spouse, your boss, your teammate, or your in-laws, there are always opportunities to see the space between stimulus and response and often when we do that, better responses occur.

Approximately six months ago, we thought my wife, Claudia, was having a heart attack. While it was a terrifying experience that turned out to be a false alarm, I did find a silver lining. My middle daughter Katie, who is thirty and has traveled the world, showed up in the emergency room, saw her mom with all sorts of monitors and tubes and at that moment, started sobbing. Through her tears, Katie told Claudia, "I just don't know what I would do if I lost you." It was this moment of beautiful grace and compassion that was the silver lining. I wouldn't wish that experience on anyone, but going through it reminded my family and I of both the fragility and sanctity of life.

I often think of this quote from Dr. Martin Luther King, Jr.: "Our character is built and revealed not in good times but in times of adversity and difficulty."

Greater resilience is a path that opens our lives to greater happiness and joy. Things like depression, isolation, exhaustion, and lack of motivation are all common, and can lead us into a downward spiral. Resilience, though, creates more capacity for us to move into an upward spiral.

How do I cultivate greater positive emotion? Well, I smile! Or I pull out a picture of my granddaughter or grandson, or call my wife or one of my daughters or my son and just say, "Hey, I'm thinking about you." My wife says I'm obsessed with exercise; I'm not, but I know what I need to keep me in an upward spiral. I always exercise first thing in the morning. In fact, I sleep in my workout clothes. That way, I can get up and go. I've been doing that for forty years. When I finish a workout, no matter what happens the rest of the day, I've accomplished something significant. That makes it easier to be in a more positive state.

These positive acts feed us. The more we can integrate these ways to maintain resilience and build joy and happiness, the more we are truly working at a higher level of realizing our fullest potential.

In Dan Buettner's book *The Blue Zones*, he writes that there are five areas in the world where people live well beyond 100 years old and live high-quality lives: the island of Sardinia; the Nicosia peninsula in Costa Rica; an enclave in California called Loma Linda; the island of Okinawa; and the Greek island of Icaria. These are temperate climates, so people are always getting sun and they're also always outside moving. There's also better access to fresh fruits and vegetables. More than that, though, the people who live in these communities place a great emphasis on family, close friends, and a shared community. Besides food and water, these are cultures of connectedness and strong social bonds, as well as places where they celebrate the importance of life and community. These are places where people are clear about what's most important in life—it's not the stuff we accumulate and acquire; it's the relationships we build and the capacity to appreciate the gift of life.

Living in paradise isn't required to be resilient. Over the last twenty years, there has been incredible research on how to recognize and treat victims of post-traumatic stress disorder and it has been a Godsend, especially in the military. Years ago, it was extremely difficult for a soldier or Marine to admit to their comrades or superiors that they were suffering from potential mental health issues such as depression and PTSD.

One of the bright spots that has emerged from all the research on PTSD is that while there is a small minority going through traumatic events like battle, divorce, terrorist attacks, and natural disasters that do develop prolonged PTSD, Jonathan Haidt and colleagues at the University of Virginia found that there are many more who experience what is now called post-traumatic growth, as they went through adverse and challenging circumstances that made them feel stronger, find hidden abilities and strengths, develop positive changes to their self-concept, strengthen good relationships, and gain greater confidence to face new challenges. The mindset, in other words, becomes: if I can survive this, I can survive anything.

Researchers now are learning so much more than ever before about what leads people down a path of post-traumatic stress disorder or post-traumatic growth. The Greek philosopher Epictetus said it well, "It's not what happens to you, but how you react to it that matters." Indeed, we are learning that mastering resilience is well within the grasp of most of us as long as we are willing to be intentional in seeing whatever adversity and difficulty we encounter in our lives as immense opportunities for growth, learning, and development, and leaning into that intention through our actions and habits to have an even more remarkable life.

THE PERCEPTION PROBLEM

Expectations aren't hardwired; we can change them. We can reprogram our negative mindsets and modify our perspectives if they are getting in the way of our well-being, joy, and happiness. His Holiness the 14th Dalai Lama was asked how he could be so joyful given that he hadn't been to Tibet, the country where he is still very much revered by the Tibetans as their spiritual leader, since he narrowly escaped the Chinese in 1959. He says what has happened does cause him immense sadness, but he has cultivated such an incredible practice of meditation that sustains his ability to maintain deep joy and peace that it has become who he is. He gets up every day at 3 a.m. to meditate for four hours.

The good news is that you and I don't need to do that.

At least, not for four hours. Meditation and mindfulness (which we'll get to in a later chapter) can help us cultivate a better perspective on our lives and problems. As we'll see later in the book, overcoming adversities can be another path toward happiness.

========== $Chapter\ 3$ ==========

HAPPINESS

Early in my adulthood, I had a mistaken view of happiness. For me, like many people, I had this idea that when I had achieved enough I could be happy. When I graduated from Harvard Business School with high distinction I knew it was quite an accomplishment. So did Claudia, who organized a celebration with friends and family. During the party, Claudia noticed I was moping around and asked what was wrong. "This is a day of celebration," she said.

My response? "But now that I've graduated from Harvard, what will people expect of me?"

That was not one of my prouder moments.

The need to accomplish, it seems, manifests itself everywhere. As a society, we are waiting to have children later and later. We want to make sure we have enough money, security, and that our professional success is well secured before we have children. But the reality is that good parenting is not a function of how much wealth, stuff, or success you have. What the research tells us over and over is that children need love, affection, and intimacy and we know that when a young child does not have these, there are significant health consequences.

I read a blog by a hospice nurse, Bonnie Ware, in which she wrote about regrets she'd heard most frequently from her dying patients over the years. Her blog, "The Top Five Regrets," went viral and became a best-selling book, *The Top Five Regrets of the Dying: A Life Transformed by the Dearly Departing.* They were:

1. I wish I'd had the courage to live a life true to myself, not the life others expected of me.
2. I wish I hadn't worked so much.
3. I wish I'd had the courage to express my feelings.
4. I wish I had stayed in touch with my friends.
5. I wish that I had let myself be happier.

What is so powerful about these regrets is that not one of them speaks to the attainment and accumulation of money or stuff. Nor are they about being more educated or having greater fame. Instead, they have to do with working less, being true to oneself, having greater friendships, and being happier. If those are the things people wish they had spent their lives attaining, why can't we be more intentional now in learning how to have more of these things in our lives?

Part of the necessary shift in our thinking is understanding what happiness is. Because as much as we chase after it, many of us have no idea what it really looks like. That certainly describes me for much of my life.

WHAT HAPPINESS IS

When we think about happiness, a lot of us have it wrong. We think that we should be living in an unrealistic state of constant euphoria—and that just isn't possible, nor should it be. Not that we won't experience those extreme highs of happiness now and then (we'll talk about that in the chapter on joy), but happiness is something simpler, and more constant.

Scientists define happiness as the experience of positive emotions and pleasure combined with deeper feelings of meaning and purpose. It's a state of being. We get to that state when we're involved in meaningful work and when we're around people we love. It's a feeling of contentment.

I have a gratitude app on my iPhone called Gratitude365. I make an entry there every day—three to five things I'm thankful for. In a future chapter I will go into greater detail regarding the importance of creating a habit of gratitude. What I want to focus on here is that part of happiness that looks back in the past, reflecting on and appreciating the good that's been in your life. You can have pride for your past and hopefulness for your future, while being present in the moment. Mystics like Eckhart Tolle would say the present moment is all we have. So much pain, suffering, and anxiety is caught up in regrets, sadness, and shame of the past. So much suffering is caused by anxiety of what's to come. So, happiness is being able to be content in all three realms—past, future, and present.

Researchers believe that we all have a defined range of our happiness "set point" and that there are generally three domains that contribute to this set point. The first domain is genetic. We all have an inevitable disposition inherited from the generations that came before us. The second domain has to do with our childhood experiences and upbringing. The culture that's created by your family matters. These two are often referred to as "nature" and "nurture," and debates often surround which of these, or how much of each, plays into our happiness and our disposition. Our level of happiness may change in temporary response to significant life events, but it then almost always returns to its baseline level as we habituate to those events and their consequences over time. Psychologists are now also telling us, however, that there is a third domain that greatly influences our happiness set point.

That third domain is how we manage our thinking. That's the one thing we have enormous power and control over. We can't change our genetic disposition and we can't undo the environment we grew up in. But we can change the way we think. Now, because of the first two domains, and the significant impact both of those can have on our lives, that doesn't mean that focusing on this third domain is easy. But it is possible, and for many of us stuck on the treadmill believing that one day when we achieve or have enough, we will be happy, it is perhaps quite necessary.

Managing our thinking isn't anything new—in fact it's been around for thousands of years. But for many of us living in a world where our brains are bombarded with information and distraction, it is hard to do. All of the world's religions try to help us develop better ways of thinking about ourselves and the people we interact with. For example, we have discussed Buddhism's four noble truths regarding suffering and impermanence. So much of human suffering comes from how we think about life, and the Buddhists believe if we can train our minds through meditation and mindfulness, we can alleviate a lot of that suffering. As shared before, the Buddhists believe that the heart of human suffering is our attachments—whatever those might be. If we can embrace this idea and begin to detach from our need to accomplish, to prove, to want more and more, then we can find greater well-being, happiness, and contentment in the present moment.

For many of us, we need to reframe our ideas of happiness. If you study some of the most successful people in the world, you'll see that happiness is a *precursor* to success, not the *result*. This illustrates how we have the achievement idea backwards. Happiness has to come first.

Shawn Anchor gave one of the most watched Ted Talks on Happiness. (Go to https://www.ted.com/talks/shawn_achor_the_happy_secret_to_better_work.) In addition to this amazing Ted Talk, he wrote the bestseller, *The Happiness Advantage,* that provides even more rich and meaningful insights about the power of being happy as a foundation for success and extraordinary joy and fulfillment in life.

In his book, he describes studies that show doctors who were in a positive mood before making a diagnosis were three times more creative and discerning and made accurate diagnoses 19 percent faster. An analysis of 200 studies on a total of 275,000 people confirmed that in almost every domain—work, friendship, health, creativity, etc.—happiness led to greater success. He even shares research that the happier we are, the healthier we are: unhappy employees stay home an average of fifteen more sick days a year!

A study of 1,306 men from 1986-1996 showed that men with the most optimistic style (one standard deviation above average) had 25 percent less cardiovascular disease than average, and men with the least optimism (one standard deviation below the mean) had 25 percent more cardiovascular disease than average. This trend was strong and continuous, indicating that greater optimism protected the men, whereas less optimism weakened them. When happy, salespeople sell more, singers sing better, artists create more, teachers teach better, coaches coach better. If you want to see a better, happier world, be happier.

CHANGING OUR MINDS

In Shawn Anchor's TED Talk, he tells a story of his little sister falling out of bed while they were playing. Being the older brother and not wanting to get in trouble, he did his best to keep her from crying. Seeing that she had landed painfully on her hands and knees, he said, "No human lands on all fours like that. Amy, I think this means you're a unicorn." It was enough to shift her perspective so that instead of crying from pain—she was instead enchanted by the idea of being a unicorn. It changed everything. Instead of crying, she went back to playing.

Why wouldn't we want to access a simple tool like that more?

Possibly because many of us don't realize we can. For a long time, I certainly didn't.

When my three oldest children were all in private universities, I took out a massive home loan to pay for it all. I was deeply resentful of that burden. I would even share my resentment with my children. I used to joke with my friends that when my kids see me, they don't see Dad, they see a wallet.

Perhaps one of my more embarrassing periods in my life was when my oldest daughter met a wonderful Frenchman in Paris, fell in love, and decided that she would have the marriage of her dreams in "Gay Paree." How wonderful...for her...not so for Dad who would have to pay for all of this. And I continually complained to any and all who would listen about how much this wedding would cost. About a week before the wedding, before we flew to France, Claudia decided that I needed a significant attitude adjustment. Essentially, her "encouraging" words were: "We are all tired of your complaining about the cost of the wedding. You had agreed to a budget and our daughter will be within the budget, so the money has been spent and you are not going to say another word about this. Instead you are going to come to France, have a grand time, and keep your complaints to yourself. If you can't do that, perhaps you shouldn't come." That was ten years ago and to this day, I am most grateful for my wife's clear direction. I did let go of my complaints about the money and I had the time of my life in France.

I'm not proud of how I mistreated my children over paying for their college costs, but over time as I worked on my own happiness I was able to shift my resentment into gratitude. Rather than see the money I had to pay, I see how incredible it is that I had the privilege of sending my children to private universities.

It has been a tremendous gift to me as my whole view on generosity has shifted; it was an area of my life that I really struggled with, and it is now an area I am proud of. Just last week, Claudia and I were looking at old pictures and letters and we found a notebook from a marriage preparation class we'd taken several months before getting married. There was an inventory of values that each of us was asked to assess in our fiancé. I was disappointed but not surprised that Claudia put down "No" regarding her assessment of my generosity. I am hopeful that she, my children, and friends might see me differently today.

While much of my coaching is in support of my clients' job performance, I also like to help my clients spend some time focusing on the importance of happiness in their lives. I'll often suggest they choose a theme for the year, a feeling they'll focus on for a whole year. So many of us get stuck in jobs that no longer bring us contentment and joy, or we find ourselves in relationships that no longer sustain us. Humans get addicted to patterns, which gives us a sense of certainty. The unknown is terrifying, and yet never changing can make us feel stuck, miserable, and certainly unhappy.

A client of mine was once struggling both in a relationship and at her job. We would talk about feeling stuck and how hard it was to get unstuck. I didn't feel like I was being very helpful. One day, I challenged her. I asked her to pick a theme for the year. She said, "Move."

I asked her what she meant. She said, "I have been stuck in a relationship, a location, and a job that no longer works for who I am and what I most desire in life. 'Move' embodies that I must have the courage and tenacity to change where I am in order to have what I want."

After several months of focusing on her theme, daily and sometimes hourly, her life began to move in extraordinary ways, and by six months, she was in a wonderful new relationship, had an offer letter for a new job, and was moving into a home with her new love in a new city. The power of intention is extraordinary. I know the "law of attraction" that what we put out into the world comes back to us in equal measure is seen by many as "new age" and a bit hokey. However, I have found in my own life that if you want to have a remarkable life, you must be clear and intentional in defining what that means and then build clear, disciplined action and habits that will keep you focused on bringing your intentions to fruition.

I recently started coaching an executive leader and told him about a great book I've read called *Ten Percent Happier* by Dan Harris. Dan was the protégé of Peter Jennings and was crushed when David Muir, one of his dear friends, was hired to fill Jennings's ABC News anchor spot instead. Dan eventually landed a spot on the ABC News religion desk. The role allowed him to interview some of the wisest and most respected spiritual leaders in the world such as Deepak Chopra, Eckart Tolle, the Dalai Lama, and Archbishop Desmond Tutu. What struck him as he learned more and more from these extraordinary people was that all of them had deep and disciplined meditation practices and he was so inspired that he started his own meditation practice.

The book describes Dan's starts and stops and how he found greater happiness as he changed his perspective toward life. He stopped some bad habits around drug use and being obsessed with achievement (at one point, he had an on-air panic attack) and started choosing to be happier. Furthermore, he used his journey to write the book that is now a best seller and even started a podcast at www.10percenthappier.com that is extremely successful. Dan turned a significant job loss into an extraordinary new career and opportunity. Given the number of people I know who have read his book or listened to his podcast focused on how to meditate and be more mindful, I am convinced he will have a much greater positive impact on the world than if he had been given Peter Jennings's job.

I am finding enormous value from Dan's insights on meditation, but I also find his 10 percent happier to be a meaningful improvement mindset. As I was sharing the book's insights with my client, I asked, "What could you do to be 10 percent happier?"

Without a pause, he said, "Improve the quality of my relationship with my wife."

There I was, coaching this man on his performance and behavior at work, and the thing he chooses is what I know is more important to him than anything else. At work, he's gotten stuck in a pattern of being tough and demanding. He has a no-nonsense approach and can be challenging in how he interacts with others. He was brave enough to share with me that this is how he can interact at home as well.

He was also brave enough to say that he knows that isn't good enough. He said he believed 10 percent was within his grasp to improve his relationship—how he listens, speaks, empathizes, and relates.

I believe that by mastering this at home, by finding greater happiness, he'll do a better job at work as well.

Dan realized what Mo Gawdat, Google Software engineer and author, says in his book, *Solve for Happy*: "Is there anything ever under our total control? Yes, two things are: your actions and your attitude.

MASTERING THE MOMENT

Happiness, again, is a state of being, that you carry with you. That doesn't mean you'll never be angry or frustrated, but it does mean that you can bring your changed perspective with you. To accomplish that, you must learn to master the moment. You must practice being content and happy in the present moment. I am reminded of the Second Splendid Truth that Gretchen Rubin writes in her best seller, *The Happiness Project*: "One of the best ways to make *yourself* happy is to make *other people* happy; and one of the best ways to make *other people* happy is to be happy *yourself.*" Think of that. It really is that simple, but only if we change our mindset of seeing our happiness as a destination instead of seeing happiness as an integral part of our life journey.

Viktor Frankl taught us that you can survive any horror by having a dream and a vision of what your life's meaning will be when you're able to escape the concentration camp or whatever difficult situation you're in. Don't let your happiness be taken away by things that you have no control over. Remember the things you're grateful for. Keep your perspective. It is about learning how to be more content and happy with the present because you know you've got a statue or painting or classroom of students waiting to be sculpted, painted, or taught. Happiness is being grateful and appreciative of the past, hopeful, optimistic, and intentional about the future, and content in the present moment.

The Dalai Lama might have said it best:

"Don't seek happiness. Be happy."

Chapter 4

JOY

As we discussed in the last chapter, we often confuse joy and happiness. We now know that happiness is more a matter of being content, a state of being we carry around with us. Joy is often what we think happiness is supposed to be. It's something more extreme and perhaps even more valuable. As I like to tell my clients, "joy is happiness on steroids."

Last year, I had the great fortune to be asked to speak at a host of physician retreats throughout the country, focusing on the topics of building greater resilience, happiness, well-being, and joy as a means to inoculate against physician burnout. The leader of one of these retreats was Dr. Avril Beckford, Chief Pediatric Officer for the WellStar Health System of Georgia. She is also on their Board of Trustees. After my talk, she excitedly told me to read the book, *The Book of Joy: Lasting Happiness in a*

Changing World, by the Dalai Lama, Archbishop Desmond Tutu, and Douglas Abrams, that chronicles a week-long conversation between these giant spiritual leaders when Tutu went to visit the Dalai Lama in India. Dr. Beckford's enthusiasm is infectious and within days I had gotten the book and digested it in one evening.

The book shows us how these men are ecstatically joyful in how they see and live in the world as they spend five days in dialogue with one another. Throughout this beautiful book, you can visualize and almost feel the love and respect these remarkable men have for each other. Here is just a taste of the wisdom these men share with each other and their readers:

"We create most of our suffering, so it should be logical that we also have the ability to create more joy. It simply depends on the attitudes, the perspectives, and the reactions we bring to situations and to our relationships with other people. When it comes to personal happiness, there is a lot that we as individuals can do."

DALAI LAMA

"Discovering more joy does not save us from the inevitability of hardship and heartbreak. In fact, we may cry more easily, but we will laugh more easily, too. Perhaps we are just more alive. Yet, as we discover more joy, we can face suffering in a way that ennobles rather than embitters. We have hard-

ship without becoming hard. We have heartbreaks without being broken."

DESMOND TUTU

While reading their conversations, I reflected on how much of their time was spent in belly-splitting laugher, and after reading the book, I realized that I don't laugh enough, certainly not at myself or with others. Only a few days after that, I had visited a client and parked my rental vehicle in a massive hospital parking garage in New Orleans. When I came back to the car, there was a note on the windshield that said, "Learn to Park Asshole!" And, well, I had earned it. I had indeed done a poor job of parking as my back tire was on the dividing line, making it difficult for any other vehicle to park next to mine. I reflected on the Dalai Lama and Desmond Tutu and just started laughing out loud, right there in the parking ramp. I now carry that note with me. Whenever I start thinking I am right or smarter than someone else, I look at that note and it always brings me joy! It keeps me grounded and never too full of myself. The person who put that beautiful note on my windshield has no idea how much I have benefited from their gift.

The Dalai Lama and Desmond Tutu's week-long encounter caused me to really reflect not just on happiness but on this elevated state of joy. Both men have experienced so much sadness and pain. Desmond Tutu was born into apartheid and became a voice of peace and joy, despite the woes and difficulties he experienced through a good portion of his life. The Dalai Lama has every right to be sad and angry, given the circumstances of the Tibetan people and that he is exiled from them. But their general state of being is joyful and their book is a calling to each of us. If we take good care of ourselves and cultivate a sense of mindfulness and "heartfulness," greater joy is possible. I found this word on the internet and heartfulness is defined as: "The fact or quality of being heartful; sincerity or warmth of feeling or expression." It's more than bliss; it's an elevated consciousness of enthusiasm, appreciation, and gratitude for life and it allows us to be much more present and in union with those around us. Perhaps Gretchen Rubin would agree with what I am calling the first Splendid Truth of Joy being, "One of the best ways to make yourself joyful is to make other people joyful; One of the best ways to make other people joyful is to be joyful yourself!"

FINDING JOY

Once you have developed the happiness habit, you will experience more joy more frequently.

So much of my joy in the past was a target to achieve. It was the same as I viewed happiness, something that came with individual achievements or successes. This is common. We think when we find love, or the kids are out of the house, or when we win the lottery, then we will experience joy. The problem too many of us have with that is we are too often miserable in the pursuit of those things—and missing opportunity for finding joy along the way.

The lesson is to not only focus on being happy, as we discussed in the last chapter but to also look for it and intentionally nurture it. And I think the key pathway is through our heart. Last month, Claudia unknowingly gave me a wonderful compliment. We were watching a few movies from a monthly subscription we have through an organization called *Spiritual Cinema*. The films, a combination of short and feature-length, all have an important message and often are inspiring and moving. At the end of the last film, Claudia said, "You cried at the end, didn't you?" I responded, "Yes, of course I did. Don't I always cry at sappy movies?"

And then she gave me the compliment: "No, when I met you at twenty-one, you didn't share your emotions very well at all. You have gotten pretty soft over the years."

I am happy for that because as I read the dialogue between the Dalai Lama and the Archbishop, they seemed so open to sharing their emotions. They are so full-hearted. I want to be more like that.

The more you open yourself up to others and embrace happiness, the more access you have to the elevated state of joyfulness. When we're happy in our pursuit, we're more likely to experience more joy, but we're also opening ourselves up to other things, other possibilities and opportunities.

Joy, for example, allows us to more deeply bond with others—and this, in turn, can lead to finding more joy in our life. My dear friend from Staten Island, John Bonviaggio, taught me that when I joined him at New York State's Arthur Kill Correctional Facility on Staten Island. My motivation was to share my gifts of music and social support with inmates, but I would inevitably leave the prison on Sunday afternoon with my own heart filled with immense joy. This was because of John's infectious joy, grace, and faith, as well as many of John's friends, who were also part of the weekend team and were such joyous and happy people.

There was an activity on Saturday night of the retreat that I still reflect on with immense joy. In the retreat room, we were organized into small table groups with equal numbers of inmates and retreat team members. Each table group received a different parable or story from the Bible, written on cards. Each group had to act out the story on their card.

One of my dearest friends, Mike Lancaster, was at the

table that needed to act out the birth of Jesus. They took a mop head from a mop and put it on one of the inmate's heads, turning him into Mary. My friend Mike was the baby. Mike is a very large man with tree trunks for legs and a massive frame. Mike took off his shirt, and his table group took a towel and tied it to him like a diaper. It was hilarious. I will never forget four guys trying to carry the giant, towel-diapered baby Jesus. Sixty people were dying of laughter for what seemed like ten minutes. I don't think I've ever laughed so hard in my life. There was a freedom about it, which is ironic, isn't it? I had come into a New York correctional facility to experience unbelievable joy, freedom, and connection with fellow humans. I couldn't have paid enough to get to be part of that joy. It's really not about a bigger house or a better car. I will carry that experience of joy with me the rest of my life. As the MasterCard commercial tells us, some things are indeed, priceless.

When you're truly in a state of joy, it is hard to be in a place of sadness or other negative emotion. I have always found it ironic that some of the greatest joy I have experienced in my life was in a spiritual retreat in a prison. I found that when I was in such a joyful state, my voices of insecurity and worthlessness disappeared. And rather than focus on the pain of the past or anxiety for an uncertain future, being joyful allowed me to be fully alive to the present.

Too often, we create distance between ourselves and

others by all this stuff in our heads about who we're supposed to be, how we can impress others, and how we can present ourselves so we will be appealing to others. When you're in the elevated state of happiness and joyfulness, I have found that much of that pretense disappears, and you can truly be present.

If you think about it, you can probably think of a few people who bring you joy just by simply being in their presence. Recently, I attended a West Point classmate's retirement from the Army Reserves, Major General (Retired) Dan York, who has been a role model for me for the last twenty-five years. In addition to serving in the military, he runs an international Christian ministry, and I'm committed to his ministry because of how he lives his life with integrity, enthusiasm, and joyfulness. But beyond being a role model, he's simply a pleasure to be around. When I'm with him, it's hard not to be joyful. He makes it easy to for me to laugh and just "be." When we're in the presence of someone who is so real, so authentic, that opens us up to joy. It's the way the Dalai Lama and Archbishop Desmond Tutu are with each other. If we weren't focused on happiness, if we didn't understand how to access the joy that comes from what we do or how we are together, we might just be two men in the same room. Instead, together, we are joyful, and when we're joyful, our bond deepens. And with a deeper bond, well, there's bound to be more joy.

The Upward Spiral by Alex Korb is a book about trying to access what Korb calls the upward spiral, which is the exact opposite of the term we're more familiar with: the downward spiral. Instead of continuing to sink lower, the book shows us how to build and grow our joy and happiness. The book does an amazing job at describing how our brains work and the impact of neurotransmitters that emit chemicals to our brain when we smile. Similarly, when we are around people with whom we don't have to pretend to be anything but ourselves and there's an ease of laughter and connection, we are elevated. Beyond smiling, laughter sparks even greater transmission of positive neurotransmitters such as serotonin and dopamine. There are some, such as the late Dr. Bernie Segal, author of *Laughter is the Greatest Medicine*, who believe that nurturing laughter actually helps us stay healthy and when ill or dealing with chronic sickness, laughter can assist in the healing and recovery process.

Happy is truly the highway to joy. We've all had the experience of peak moments in our life of immense joy, and sometimes it takes effort to make sure those are the memories that stay front and center. I know I keep images in my mind of key moments: seeing my bride walk down the aisle at Holy Trinity Chapel at West Point; being present at the safe and healthy delivery of our first child, Emily; graduating from US Army Ranger School with my brother and hero pinning my Ranger Tab on my shoulder; taking

Claudia to an amazing resort for our twenty-fifth wedding anniversary with a catered dinner on the beach; and, of course, hundreds more. There's a part of us that is always trying to find these peak experiences. And I know even in the moments that I am vividly remembering these wonderful memories, there are feelings of joy that are unhindered by any negative emotions such as fear, anxiety, anger, and sadness. If we are intentional about choosing happiness, we have greater access to the even more powerful emotional state of joy.

JOY EXISTS IN THE PRESENT

If you have gotten this far, you should be quite familiar with my story of living from a place of never being content. Happiness, I told myself, would come one day when I had enough and when I was enough. Part of the path to joy is a recognition and intention about living in the present moment. The more we can be present and the more we can be intentional about the fact that this moment is all we have, the happier and more joyful we will be.

I was reminded of this just several months ago, when Claudia and I were watching Estelle. She was screaming about something, and I went into her room. Rather than be angry or frustrated about her current state, I chose to have a calm, non-anxious, and loving presence. I had a smile on my face and tried to reflect warmth and peace.

As I held her in my arms, I let go of any tension, concerns, or expectations that Estelle should be anything other than what she was at the very moment. And what was amazing was how quickly she stopped screaming and calmed down as well. We read a story, and then she happily climbed into her crib and said, "Goodnight Poppy." I wish that this was a more common experience in my life, and I assure you that with my own children, I am not sure I had the insight nor the inclination to be so present to let go of past guilt or future anxiety and just be. But I'm now glad I cultivated that ability and can share it with other parents in addition to being a better grandfather.

There is an extraordinary book I read years ago by a very prominent Rabbi and scholar, Edwin Friedman, that speaks of the impact one could have on their family, community, and workplace by just maintaining what Rabbi Friedman referred to as "a non-anxious presence." The name of the book is, *Leadership and a Failure of Nerve in the Age of the Quick Fix*, and perhaps one of the most powerful quotes was:

> "*Differentiation 'is the capacity to take a stand in an intense emotional system.' It enables us to resist polarizing forces and maintain a non-anxious presence in an anxious system, and not allow ourselves to become one of the system's 'emotional dominoes.' It enables us to recognize where we end and others begin, and to have*

clearly defined personal values, boundaries, and goals.
Differentiation enables us to take the maximum amount
of responsibility for our being and destiny."

It seems to me that my encounters with people like Kempton Haynes and John Bonviaggio have given me the insight and support to discover the beginnings of this concept of "differentiation" and to have greater tools so I might "resist polarizing forces" and not let other's emotional trauma become my own. Being comfortable in the present moment is another great tool to build differentiation.

Not only do we need to be intentional about seeing happiness as the pathway to joy, but we need to be deliberate about doing things that make us happier and taking advantage of the opportunities for joy in the present moment—even when (or especially when) that comes in the form of something like a screaming child.

For example, a client of mine recently took one of her children to college. Now, she has weekends that are freer than before, but she isn't intentional about using that time to do things that bring her joy and happiness. Instead, she spends too much time missing her daughter. I asked her to think about the things that bring her joy. For me, it's playing piano. When I'm in my music room, playing and singing, I'm not thinking about the future or the past. I'm completely present. For some people, it's running. For others, it's riding a horse. For some, it's riding on their power mower. We need to be intentional about creating space for the things that give us greater happiness and joy. I challenged my client to be more intentional about bringing greater joy to her life, and recently she showed me a picture of her riding her horse and how she is making that a weekly practice. As she was sharing the picture, you could sense her positive energy through her big, warm smile.

Remember, joy is infectious. When we are around people who are in a state of relaxation and authentic, unpretentious joy, it's hard not to feel the same way. To be human is to want those things. We live several houses down from a daycare center and for most of the late afternoon if the weather is reasonably good, you hear a symphony of young, happy, screaming voices coming from the daycare center playground. I love to walk by the center just to hear that beautiful sound of young children who have not yet been burdened down by their thinking of how hard or difficult life is or will be. Instead, they are being free, authentic, and open to the joys of life. How can we find our way back to that place from time to time? Certainly, the Dalai Lama and Desmond Tutu do it with great ease, and we can, too.

FINDING JOY WHEN IT'S TOUGH

One of my clients, Dr. Richard Guthrie, is the chief quality officer of Ochsner Health System in Louisiana and he often emphasizes that the normal state of human beings is psychological fear. He makes this point because it underscores the difficulty and importance that healthcare organizations can have in creating psychological safety for others. Too often our state of being is to be in a perpetual state of anxiety. It's deeply wired in our genetics. It's a survival and self-protection mechanism. And if unchecked it can cause us to suffer from chronic stress, burnout, and unhappiness. As I have written previously, there are circumstances in our lives that warrant being highly vigilant. However, the majority of human beings living in America no longer have to live their lives in high fear and perpetual anxiety. And when we do find ourselves in challenging and stressful conditions, being joyful and happy regardless of the circumstances around us can actually help us cope and perform better. Not only can we find joy during the toughest times, it's also important to recognize that joy might be what gets us through those tough times.

When I was a young captain in the Army stationed at Ft. Bragg, North Carolina, and serving in the 82nd Airborne Division, I had the privilege of working for extraordinary leaders who went on to senior command positions throughout the Army. One of the most inspiring was General Buck Kernan, who was a Lieutenant Colonel when we served together. I can recall on multiple occasions when things got very tough and tense that he would use humor, sarcasm, and laughter as tools to help all of us manage better through the stress. There was a training exercise where our battalion jumped close to fields occupied by buffalo. He had our personnel officer "secure" a dried piece of buffalo dung and when the exercise was over, had it shellacked and glued to a plaque. Each month we would have a dinner for all the officers in the battalion and inevitably that plaque would be awarded to the officer who demonstrated the most "bone-headed" mistake or shortcoming during the month. (I am pretty sure I won that award of distinction several times.) We can find joy when it's tough. And, as we can see from my Staten Island prison experience, we can find joy in the most unexpected of places.

I remember discussing this with a client of mine, Jeff, who has a young family, has some tremendous health challenges, and is in a role in an industry that has gotten significantly more difficult and regulated. He told me he has come to be bored by what he does. Because there was a lack of checks and balances in his industry, there is so much more bureaucracy and regulation now that has taken much of the fun out of it for Jeff. He no longer feels challenged or emotionally charged about his former hopes and dreams for the field.

Needless to say, he does not experience too many spikes of joy in his work life.

I asked him, "What can we do about this?" One option, I said, is to leave. Another option is to figure out how to be more joyful and happy at a job that is no longer as fun and exciting as it used to be. We spoke about Jeff's strengths and how he might better leverage those throughout each day. Research shows us that when we use our strengths more frequently, we are happier and we tend to perform better. That was important for him to remember, that finding more joy in his life was a choice. We also spoke a lot about perspective and remembering to compare our situation with those who are in much more perilous, difficult, challenging, harsh environments. I shared my photo of the two Nigerian girls and we spoke about the opportunities Jeff had each day to make a positive difference in the lives of others. As *The Upward Spiral* teaches us, creating a positive, virtuous cycle is often much easier than we think and all that is required is one moment of joy to jumpstart our own upward spiral.

Jeff is not alone. Here's some of the latest data on the US workplace. As of 2017:

- Gallup reported that 51 percent of the US workforce is not engaged, while only 16 percent of employees said they felt "connected and engaged" by employers.
- Gallup also reported that 51 percent of workers are looking to leave their current job and that only 42 percent of public school superintendents in the US are engaged with their jobs.

- Hays Consulting reported that 54 percent of employees are very unhappy in their current role while 84 percent of employees would consider leaving their current role for the right offer.

So, Jeff, like many other Americans, doesn't find much joy in his work—but we can also carve out places of joy at work if we become intentional and get a little creative. As I have written several times, we don't see the world as it is but see it as we are. If we are in a state of hating our job, such dissatisfaction begins to color everything. The key is focusing on the parts of a job that you love, the parts that let you use your strengths (in other words, cultivating happiness, as we discussed in the last chapter).

Research from Gallup says we feel more joyful when we are doing work consistent with our strengths, so when we are using talents that come naturally we tend to be more satisfied, productive, and successful. One of my greatest strengths is that I am a maximizer, which means I'm constantly looking for ways things can be better. I'll ask clients: What can you do to be 10 percent happier? Or 10 percent more joyful? Or 10 percent more productive? For most of us, 10 percent is not out of the realm of possibility. Only a few weeks ago, a client shared that they used the 10 percent happier question over their Christmas holidays and it made a big difference in their disposition and interactions with others. And their improved happiness greatly improved mine because I was able to use a strength to help another human being improve their lives.

Another of my strengths is positivity. When I coach my clients, I am very intentional about showing up with a positive attitude centered on helping them make their lives better. And as I have gotten more intentional about using this strength of positivity, it gets stronger and plays more of a part in improving the quality of the interactions I have with my clients.

One of the core elements I coach and teach regarding making teams and relationships more effective is that by keeping our positive to negative interactions as high as possible, we promote higher cohesion and more effective communication. Psychologist Barbara Fredrickson from the University of Maryland, and her colleague Marcial Losada from Chile, originally outlined their "positivity calculus" theory in a 2005 paper published in the journal *American Psychologist*. In it, they suggest that flourishing is associated with positivity ratios of about three-to-one and that a more common ratio of two-to-one could help people "get by," but not thrive.

Further research on high performing teams pointed to an average of 5.6 positive interactions for every negative one. The 19 low-performance teams racked up a positive/negative ratio of just .363. That is, they had about three negative interactions for every positive one. John Gottman, whom many consider one of the masters of effective marriages and relationships, has said couples with a ratio of fewer than five positive interactions for every negative one, are destined for divorce.

I find that by using my strength of positivity, I increase the connection and effectiveness of my relationships, while also increasing my personal satisfaction. There is an abundance of research from Gallup as well that the more you utilize your strengths, the more satisfied you are. Jeff has five top strengths, so we've been talking about what he can do to make sure he uses those strengths every day. The job itself may not be as exciting or fulfilling as it once was, but he can find greater fulfillment from using his strengths. For him, that's been enormously helpful.

Jeff's top strength is individualization; he has a gift for helping people who are different work together well. He has a team of people he's responsible for, and when he coaches them, he uses this skill, which, in turn, feels fulfilling to him.

Competition is another one of his top strengths, and so he initiated a competition around the office to see who could lose the most weight. He's not just cultivating another habit, movement, which we'll discuss later, but he's found a way to make it joyful.

This results in Jeff's spikes of joy, which keeps the happiness rolling.

I bet you've experienced joy in unexpected places, perhaps without realizing it. When a loved one has a health scare, for example, we draw together and reach out to feel one another's pain and to help each other through it. Many funerals have a wake, which allows family and friends to reflect and feel the family's pain and hardship. It also allows the community to embrace the family and let them know their loved one won't be forgotten. In these intense moments of pain, we also sometimes find joy. And when we realize this, we're better equipped to experience it next time, and to help others experience it as well.

The last several years of my life have been some of the most happy and joyful and not because I have accomplished more or anything significant changed in what was happening in my life. Instead, my attitude has changed and I see that every day is an opportunity to choose to be joyful and happy.

As I have shared several times previously, I grew up with intense insecurity from hearing the voices in my head say over and over that I was a mistake and certainly not enough. I recognize now that these voices were designed to protect me from harm and to propel me to seek the attention and appreciation of others so that the insecurities could be silenced for at least awhile. Now, many of the voices of insecurity and doubt I used to have are just old friends and when they come, I welcome them with appreciation for what they were and then allow them to go on their way, since I don't need them anymore to protect me. I believe this wonderful change in my life has come about because of the disciplines I've followed in terms of my own sense of being grateful and of perspective. The more we can access happiness and joy in the present moment, the more it allows us to put fear and anxiety aside. We don't have to be depressed. We don't have to have an epidemic of drug abuse. There are better ways to live our lives. We just have to be intentional about using the tools and techniques that can help us truly be our best selves.

Chapter 5

LIVING WITH PURPOSE

Randall Jones is the Chief Medical Officer of a healthcare company that provides emergency medicine and hospitalist physicians to hospitals across the nation. When we started working together, his company was experiencing a surge of growth and many challenges associated with that growth. At one point earlier in the company's history, Randall had been the company's president and he had stayed on as Chief Medical Officer after he and his cofounders sold the company to a shrewd and strongly business-focused organization. That organization felt that with the right financial management and control systems, the healthcare organization could be much more profitable than it had been. The people running Randy's company were great at what they did—growing businesses. But Randy was a physician, and only one of two remaining among the most senior executives. Given that the new owners and senior executives were most focused on getting the organization on firm financial footing, Randall was worried about the direction of his company and staying true to their mission of providing appropriate clinical leadership through the work of thousands of physicians. However, given his current environment, it would be easy for him to get caught up in the business of the business.

He is an emergency medicine physician himself, who still practices and maintains his board certifications. He has always identified as a doctor. His struggle was finding a new purpose in an organization that had essentially been his to run for a long time. But it was proving tough. He was too caught up in the business side of things and was no longer the one calling the shots.

So, I told him about the role of the water carrier within some Native American cultures.

From popular culture, we know about many roles in the Native American communities—the chief, the medicine man, and so forth. But one we don't often hear of is the one known as the water carrier. The role of the water carrier was to pass down the values, history, and traditions of the tribe through storytelling, so that the tribe's culture and true essence was never lost and forgotten.

I suggested to Randall, as the Chief Medical Officer, that he was the de facto water carrier of the company.

It takes a lot for a human being to step down from the most senior leadership role and see something that has been your baby now be run by someone else. But Randall has taken great pride in his water carrier role, reminding his colleagues and employees that the essence of the organization is taking care of physicians so they can take care of patients. His purpose changed, but he found a new one.

Psychologically, it may have been easier for Randall to find another job at a different organization. But he was committed to this company that he had played such a significant role in building, and found a purpose as the most senior executive who was actually a physician. Rather than this being a burden, it became an opportunity and a responsibility—and ultimately a mighty purpose. He knew he had to be as knowledgeable and capable as the new business leaders surrounding him to hold his own. He found what was unique about his role and embraced his purpose of making sure the company never lost its essence of being patient-centered and physician-driven.

The medical director role is critical, and it's one of the things that has helped the company maintain its competitive advantage. Good clinical leadership in demanding circumstances is key, and through finding his own purpose,

Randall was able to remind others what they're there to do and collaborate in their shared purpose. He's never forgotten his roots. He is always able to put himself in the shoes of a serving and practicing physician. He strives to stay mindful of what life looks like from their vantage point.

Through the water carrier story I discussed with Randall, he found his work to be suddenly even more important than ever.

FINDING PURPOSE

In the book *Good to Great* by Jim Collins, he talks about the hedgehog concept. He looked at 1,500 companies over a certain period of time and found that only 11 made the jump from being good to great. "Greatness" was defined as financial performance several multiples better than the market average over a sustained period. Collins found the main reason certain companies become great is they narrowly focus the company's resources on their few key and dominant competencies and apply those competencies toward a mighty purpose.

The leaders of these eleven companies weren't well-known public figures, as many of them avoided the limelight and had introverted tendencies. In addition, they each had two dominant qualities. The first was deep personal humility. Success was never about them; they never needed to have glory focused on themselves. The second quality was a great sense of collective purpose for their organization and an immense determination to achieve that purpose.

The hedgehog is an animal that, when it gets its teeth into something, never lets go. The eleven companies that made the journey from good to great had great tenacity and clarity of purpose that focused the organization's attention despite whatever adversity or distractions came their way, just like the hedgehog when it gets its teeth into something.

The hedgehog was Collins's way of trying to clarify how they found that mighty purpose, using three overlapping circles. The first circle was identifying what these great companies were most passionate about. The second circle was fully understanding what they could be really great at; and the third circle was being clear on what would drive their economic engine to its fullest extent.

Many years ago, I had the privilege of listening to Jim Collins speak on his book at a leadership conference at the United States Military Academy. While the conference was for business leaders, the Academy and Jim thought it would be a great idea if West Point Cadets were invited to his keynote presentation. And when he shared the Hedgehog Concept with the audience, he was deliberate in changing the third circle question from, "What drives your economic engine?" to "Where can you have your greatest impact and do your greatest good?" He also shared a delightful story about a conversation that the famous management guru and his mentor, Peter Drucker, had with him when they were both on the faculty at Stanford Business School. "Mr. Collins, you always seem so worried about making money. You're so gifted and talented. You should never have to worry about that. What you need to be most worried about, given that all of us have a fixed amount of time on this earth, is where is the place you can do your greatest good and be true to that."

That clearly made such an impact on Collins that he modified how he defined his third circle. Given that a large portion of the audience were West Point Cadets who would graduate and go on to lead young women and men willing to put themselves in harm's way in defense of America's security, it also made great sense to them. And it should modify all of our third circles. When it's about more than money, we're better, happier people. I attended that conference at least fifteen years ago and Collins's words still inspire and educate me.

I continue to use modifications of Jim Collin's three concentric circles with many of my clients when we are working to clarify their mighty purpose, asking them these three questions:

- What are you most passionate in this world about accomplishing and achieving?
- What have life's experiences, your education, temperament, and talent best equipped you to do better than most?
- Where can you have your greatest impact and do your greatest good in this one, precious life?

When one gets clarity regarding the answers to these three questions, I have found it to be an effective path toward defining and clarifying one's purpose. As Jim Collins would say, in the place where the three concentric circles overlap, you will find your hedgehog and if one stays true, focused, and persistent toward that center, you will have a life that is impactful, meaningful, and fulfilling.

I highly recommend a TED presentation to my clients entitled: *How Great Leaders Inspire Action* by Simon Sinek. The presentation is listed as the third most popular TED presentation and you can view it by going to: https://www.ted.com/talks/simon_sinek_how_great_leaders_inspire_action

In the presentation, Sinek talks about (also using a diagram of circles) why Apple is such a successful company. He says Apple is brilliant as an innovator because it has been able to get clear as to its mighty "why." Just like Dell and HP, they started out as a company that created and sold computers and most of their marketing messages focused on what they did and how they did it better than their competitors. However, like most inspiring leaders and great companies, Apple starts with addressing that they believe in challenging the status quo and their products whether they be computers, phones, or music players and Apple continues to challenge the status quo with every product they put out into the market. When they created and released the iPhone, their "why" wasn't to make a better phone (what). No, it was to transform people's lives (why). The "why" is your purpose. It's your reason for doing what you do. When you have a powerful "why," any "what" is achievable.

STUMBLING INTO PURPOSE

The Gallup strengths finder has thirty-four strengths. Their research states there is a 1 in 37 million chance someone else will have the top 5 strengths in the same order as you. My thirty-fourth strength is being deliberate. Gallup would tell me that being deliberate is not something that God put in me and so I've winged a lot in my life, especially in finding my purpose. If someone would have told me thirty-seven years ago when I graduated from West Point that I would be spending most of my time having one-on-one conversations with people about their lives, I would have said, "You're crazy! Why would people pay me and how could I ever be happy doing that?!"

While I have a calling and profession as an executive coach and leadership educator that I have deeply loved for the last sixteen years, I have to admit that I stumbled into my purpose. I was an infantry officer with seven years of active service in elite Airborne infantry units when the United States Military Academy contacted me indicating their desire for me to consider teaching at West Point for several years as a rotational Army assignment. As part of that assignment, they would allow me to go to graduate school for two years to attain my master's degree with any related subject to what I might teach in.

I didn't know if I would like teaching or if I would be any good at it. I had been hand selected to transfer from the 82nd Airborne Division to serving in the Army Ranger Regiment, an even more elite and prestigious assignment, and it was something that previously had been an important career ambition for me. As I reflected on the decision to give up the Ranger assignment and instead teach at West Point, I am not sure my life's purpose was as clear as it is now. So, I thought about how demanding the military life had been, especially on my wife and our young family of three toddlers, as I considered the opportunities that might open for me by getting a master's degree in a terrific school and in getting experience teaching Cadets at West Point.

Additionally, my older brother, Captain Donald Hiebert,

had died only a few years earlier in a B-52 crash with the rest of his crew, as well as his group commander on a high peak in southwestern Utah. It was a terrible accident and my brother's death, to this day, was one of the most difficult events of my life and the lives of all of my siblings and parents.

Don Hiebert was perhaps one of the most extraordinary human beings my other four siblings and I had ever encountered in our lives. When I proposed to Claudia in the spring of my senior year at West Point, my parents told me that it was a very poor decision to get married at such a young age and they would not actively support our upcoming wedding. But my older brother was incredibly supportive and excited for me. He agreed to be my best man at the wedding and I could not have been prouder or more honored when he asked me to be his best man at his wedding seven months later.

My brother had this unique gift of seeing me not as I saw myself, "the unlovable, worthless failure" but seeing me as good, successful, and gifted. He had always wanted to be a teacher and had hoped to be selected by the Air Force at some point in his career to teach at the United States Air Force Academy, his alma mater. The world lost a great man when he died, and I try to honor his life by frequently asking myself, "What would Dee (my brother's nickname) do in this situation?" I asked this question in regard to this big career decision and I heard the answer quite clearly: "Go teach."

So, I took the plunge, turned down the Ranger assignment, and called West Point to let them know I would take the opportunity to teach leadership. In retrospect, that decision greatly changed not just the trajectory of my life but also set me on a journey of purpose and calling that continues passionately to this day. At Claudia's urging, I decided to apply to Harvard Business School. I thought there wasn't a chance I would ever get in. Thankfully, my wife has always been a stronger believer in me than I was, and she was quick to say, "Well, you will never get in if you never apply, so what have you got to lose?" On the application, one of the essay questions was, "What are your hobbies?" As I indicated previously, we had three toddlers to include twins who were not yet two. In response to that question I described "the art and science of changing diapers." The admissions committee either had such a chuckle or felt such deep pity for me that I was awarded admission.

I went through two incredible years at Harvard Business School and then showed up at West Point. My department had a two-month teaching process where they would help us become good teachers. It was transformational. It was scary, too, because you had to plan classes and teach them, videotaping yourself and then watching the tapes with your peers and they were tough and demanding. But I came to find out that I loved teaching. It continues to be one of my greatest joys in life.

After three years of teaching at West Point, the Army had other plans for me that would entail several more moves with my young family. I also came to realize that I would have loved to teach full-time but couldn't figure out how I could make that happen with my young family. My destiny was no longer in the Army. I made another difficult decision to find my path outside of a structure that had been a part of my life since birth. (My father had fulfilled a thirty-three-year career in the Army.)

I was fortunate while on the faculty at West Point to be introduced to McKinsey and Company, a premier strategic consulting company that had offices around the globe, which included, at the time, a dozen or so offices in the United States. After going through fifteen interviews, I found myself excited by the possibility of being a McKinsey consultant and received an offer to join their Atlanta Office. And while McKinsey would open further doors and opportunities for me, I was still uncertain as to what my purpose in life was. However, the seeds of leadership development had been planted as a teacher at West Point, and at McKinsey, I felt drawn back into the domain of leadership and seeing its impact, good and bad, as a key contributor to organizational effectiveness and success.

As I later left consulting and got into an operational role at BellSouth, one of my McKinsey clients, I continued to be pulled back into leadership development. I put together frameworks regarding transformational and servant leadership, and whenever I had the opportunity, I would teach and present on themes of leadership effectiveness. With responsibility for the success of twenty customer sales and service call centers throughout the Southeast, I created a small team called the Leadership Assistance Team. The team was comprised of several exceptional leaders who had been taught and coached to go into the call centers to greatly inspire higher employee performance and engagement. It was a great success and for this and other innovations, I received several awards for my work on teaching and coaching leadership. I started to realize that perhaps this was what I was meant to do with the rest of my life.

It was then I began to ponder with greater intensity what it would be like if I taught and consulted on leadership as a full-time profession. I only wish at the time I had the hindsight to have used Jim Collins's Hedgehog framework, as I think I could have greatly accelerated my efforts to get clarity around my life's purpose.

However, slowly, that clarity began to get focused as I realized that my strengths were aligned with teaching one-on-one, meeting each person where they were, helping them in figuring out their strengths, and then helping them discover insights and develop new commitments that would make them more effective, happy, joyful, and resilient. While it took several more years of stumbling and fumbling in my professional journey, as my life's purpose began to take shape, I was drawn to it and could not let it go.

PURPOSE AND INTENTION

It's easy to get pulled by the winds of life. Many people never reflect on why they're doing what they're doing. When I meet a client for the first time, I always love for them to share their "story" about how they came to be in front of me to include the early choices they made in their lives regarding education, friends, hobbies, and skills, as well as the factors that influenced their lives such as where they lived, their parents' professions, their birth order, and influence of siblings, teachers, and other family members. I am always amazed by people's stories and how so many end up in professions or certainly taking professional paths by circumstance and unplanned or unanticipated opportunities, as happened to me.

I have been an avid reader and student of Jim Collins's books and research for many years to include being inspired by his first bestseller, *Built to Last*. Another meaningful and impactful book is *Great by Choice*. In this book, like in his other bestsellers, he uses rigorous research methods to get at well-supported truths and insights, and I probably reflect on one of his most significant insights from the book at least weekly, "Greatness is not a function of circumstance. Greatness, it turns out, is a matter of conscious choice and discipline."

Think about the implications of Collins' conclusion. For me, it says that being great is open to all of us, but it must begin with clear intention followed by incredibly hard and disciplined effort and persistence. I have always found it amazing that many of the most exceptionally successful people in the world dropped out of school or did not obtain educational credentials. Bill Gates is one of the most famous and dropped out of Harvard, while Steve Jobs dropped out of Reed College. I have come to believe that sometimes too much education can be a dangerous thing, especially if it tempers your dreams and the courage of your aspirations. Please don't misunderstand me. I don't think education is a bad thing, as it has certainly opened many doors and opportunities for me, but sometimes dreaming and achieving greatness requires a boldness and willingness to overcome conventional thinking and mental models, while many educational programs teach and reinforce conventional wisdom and rationalization.

I have found in my own journey, reinforced by solid research from pioneers like Jim Collins, that the more intentional we can be in our lives, the more we can create lives of significance and meaning. Just the other day, I asked a client if they had goals or aspirations outside of their professional lives. For example, do they create meaningful goals regarding the quality of relationships they have with their spouse, children, extended family, or friends? It was clear to me that they did not see the significance of that since they felt that setting goals for their professional lives was sufficient and hard enough. My response, though, was that perhaps in the most precious things in their lives, like the quality of their relationships with those they loved, creating and tracking goals was even more important.

I love the C.S. Lewis quote: "People need to be reminded more often than they need to be instructed." Remember, our thinking brain, the prefrontal cortex, is highly limited and easily diminished by fatigue and stress. It's impossible to think of and remember everything we need throughout our busy days, even if you read all the time or know a lot about science. We just don't have an efficient retrieval system. If you can remind yourself and others of important virtues or qualities to focus on for the day, it makes it easier to stay on the path to joy.

Every day, I try to be intentional about what my purpose is, what values I want to live by and embody to achieve that purpose, and reflect on the key priorities that will bring me closer to achieving my purpose. Left to my own devices and memory, it would be very easy to forget to reflect on what is most important in my life.

Approximately four years ago, I realized that I was not disciplined enough in living out my purpose, principles, and priorities. One of my insights was that I tend to wing things far too much and that the Army provided me with instant structure and organization that, left to my own devices, I probably would not have. In the Army, there was a format, template, and standing operating procedure for just about everything. You can imagine how, when you are in dangerous and intense situations, it is helpful to have sound structures and operating procedures that can guide people to be focused, clear, and as on task as possible. When I left the military, I found that I really missed the Army structures I had become accustomed to.

By starting my day with an early morning ritual around being purposeful and clear around my principles, priorities, and the people that I needed to work, interact, and communicate with, I tended to be more focused and intentional throughout the day. That prompted me to create a tool called "The 6Ps for Profound and Positive Living." When I realized that I could have a framework where I would reflect on key words that started with the letter P, beginning with Purpose, that would be useful to make my day as intentional and focused as possible, it naturally flowed from Purpose to other "Ps."

The other Ps I developed were Principles, Priorities, People, Perspective, and Presence. I found that the more I used the tool, the higher the probability that my day would be much more positive and profound. As I made it a key habit of most days, I realized that it was something I could share with clients and friends, and over the last several years, I have received great feedback that others have also found the tool to be useful in helping them stay clear, focused, and disciplined in their daily lives.

Here is a sample of the worksheet I use and share with clients:

WORKSHEET-6 P'S FOR PROFOUND
AND POSITIVE LIVING
Make this an early morning ritual (EMR) and Review Daily:

- **P1-Purpose:** How can I ensure that this day is filled with significance, meaning, and passion? My coaching and teaching purpose: remember that my primary purpose as a coach, educator, and facilitator is to connect with others in trust, appreciation, and understanding and to leverage that connection to support their efforts to be effective, productive, engaged, and successful in all facets of their lives.

- **P2-Principles for Living:** How can I stay centered on a few powerful and poignant principles? (I use the acronym CHICK to remember my five principles below.)
  - Compassion and Empathy-Everyone's life has struggle and heartache; how can I fully appreciate what others are experiencing and provide a place of refuge and support for them in the midst of whatever challenges and difficulties they may be going through?
  - Humility—In my time with others, what matters most is serving and supporting them; what do they need? What do they aspire to? What are their obstacles and barriers? What are their talents and strengths?
  - Integrity- This is about seeing our work lives as integrated with all the other elements of our lives and integration of what we live, with what we espouse. How can I help others gain greater insight into their own integrity and how they might see opportunities to strengthen that?
  - Courage-Sometimes the best I can do for someone is to facilitate dialogue that may be uncomfortable and that requires me to be courageous in creating some tension and discord.
  - Kindness-Every human being regardless of ethnicity, geographic origins, and social economic conditions will encounter sorrow, pain, and dis-

appointment at one point in their lives. One of the ways I can serve others is to extend to them as much kindness as possible. It is easy to render, and one never knows the positive and uplifting impact it may have on them.

- **P3-Priorities for this day:** Given my purpose and principles, what are the very most important things I must accomplish to maximize this day and move me closer to my goals?

- **P4-People:** Who in my life do I need to touch, affirm, support, challenge, and connect with beyond the meetings I have currently scheduled for this day?

- **P5-Perspective:** Life presents challenges to us all and yet it is far too easy to let the small and insignificant things dampen our joy and happiness. Perspective is a powerful tool to reflect that our life's difficulties are relatively small in comparison to those who are suffering immensely from harsh realities such as civil war, famine, starvation, violence, and brutality. Often, our woes and difficulties, when compared with these, are insignificant and can warrant an appreciation for the lives we do have.

- **P6-Presence:** All we really have is this present moment. The past cannot be undone or relived, and the future is yet before us. How can we be fully present to each and every present moment and make that moment as meaningful as possible? Presence is a powerful tool for us to remember to be ever present to the now of this moment. And research has shown us that several tools can enhance and support our efforts to be present:

- Gratitude: Taking a moment each day to reflect on the blessings in our lives and to be grateful for these blessings can be a powerful enabler of our joy and happiness.
- Movement: Our bodies were designed for movement and research has shown that as we age, maintaining a balance of aerobic and strength workouts can slow down the natural decay of not just our bodies, but also our minds.
- Mindfulness: Research only increases regarding the positive impacts on our mental, emotional, and even physical well-being of a daily meditation practice where we are disciplining our minds to slow down, focus, and even be quiet and still.
- Prayer: Regardless of our religious affiliation or disposition, prayer is a means to intentionally connect with the divine in whatever form we experience it and to connect and ground ourselves with that divine force. Sometimes asking for divine intervention for our family, friends, community, and ourselves can bring us greater peace and allows for us to be more open to the present moment.

I have found that when I take the time to go through the 6 Ps before my day starts, I am amazingly centered and focused, and it is a habitual way to connect me with my purpose as well as how I want to conduct myself in order to pursue that purpose.

PURPOSE IS LONG-TERM

How can we find our purpose? I have found through my coaching and teaching that there are some core questions that have been truly beneficial for others in helping them find their purpose and deeper meaning in their lives. Some of the big questions I love to ask are:

- What do you want people to say about you when you're gone?
- When do you feel most alive?
- What is your life calling you to be?
- What have you been put here on earth to do?
- What activities give you great meaning in your life?

Another way to have people engage in their meaning and purpose is to have them reflect on the end of their lives, when someone is asked to give the eulogy at their funeral. What is it that you would want others to honestly and authentically say about you and about the impact you have had on others? I have found that by writing our own eulogy with integrity and intention, it can be an extremely powerful tool to get clear about the life you have and how to live it as fully as possible.

In my own eulogy, there are five dominant virtues and qualities that I want my friends and family to think of when they reflect on my life. Purposely, most of these qualities overlap with some of the principles I center myself on in my coaching and teaching. These core virtues are: compassion, humility, kindness, generosity, and being purposeful. I came to these five qualities through my own reflection on the qualities of those I admired most in the world and who I wanted to most emulate.

After I chose those five qualities that I wanted to be remembered for, I also reflected on what it would take for these qualities to truly reflect what others came to see in me. And honestly, most of these qualities are quite challenging for me. As I reflect on Collins's quote, "Greatness, it turns out, is a matter of conscious choice and discipline," I have taken the first step in consciously choosing these five qualities as a core reflection of who I aspire to be. I know then I must create and live a disciplined process with great determination and persistence if there is any possibility of truly reflecting these qualities.

Take generosity. It's the kind of thing we'd like to think is easy, but for me that certainly isn't the case. My parents lived through the depression and my mother in particular was extremely frugal and passed on that frugality to me. I have often lived from a place of scarcity instead of abundance and the mindset of, if I give you something I have, I no longer have it for my own. And it is really hard to give when you live from a place where you don't have enough and aren't enough. But becoming more generous has become very important to me. I've mentioned how reluctant I was to pay for my kids' college and how I would take every opportunity I could to remind them how much of a financial drain they were. Obviously, that wasn't very generous. It takes work and deliberate choice for me to put that part of my purpose into practice. Oh, by the way, when you live from a place of abundance instead of scarcity, you also experience much less anxiety and open yourself up to even more joy and happiness.

My wonderful friend, John Bonviaggio, of course had something significant to say about this using a quote from Bud Wainscott, "What you keep you lose, but what you give away is yours forever." Think about the power and truth of that quote. There are no U-hauls behind the hearses and we cannot take all the stuff we accumulate with us when we die. However, when we live from a place of deep generosity, the impact of our lives on others is magnified and passed on to those we have been generous to.

THE RESULTS OF PURPOSE

Whatever we feed grows. The more we focus on something, the more it manifests in our lives. I often reference one of the greatest self-help books ever written, *Think and Grow Rich* by Napoleon Hill. Hill was a young man when he met Andrew Carnegie, who was at the time the richest man in the world.

Carnegie was impressed by Hill and his quest for greatness. He asked him to study the most successful people in the world and determine their qualities and traits that allow them to be successful. Carnegie told Hill that he wasn't going to pay him for the work but that he would open up to him something of greater value, his network of some of the most successful and accomplished people in the world.

Hill eagerly took up Carnegie's challenge and studied success and the most wildly successful for many years. Many of his discoveries and conclusions are contained in Hill's *Think and Grow Rich*. Rich doesn't refer to money, but is about a life rich in success. After studying thousands of successful people, as well as the lives of many unsuccessful people, Hill observed three dominant qualities that were present in the most successful. The first was that the successful people had a vivid, compelling sense of purpose and direction. The second was that they were able to focus their attention on that purpose, ignoring distractions and obstacles. The third was that they had a tenacity and persistence about them; they would never give up until their purpose had been achieved. I have shared that message with thousands of others because it is simple and quite similar to Jim Collins's quote on greatness. It opens up the possibility of greatness to all of us if we are intentional in having a compelling purpose in our lives and we are disciplined and determined to stay at this purpose over and over regardless of the distractions, challenges, and difficulties that show up in our lives.

I've never found anything that conflicts with those three qualities.

So, yes, whatever you're paying attention to manifests. But you need the discipline to stay true and attentive to the purpose, not the distractions.

And distractions are everywhere in today's world. With smart phones and social media and e-mail and the 24-hour news cycle, it's hard not to be distracted. It takes even greater discipline today to stay true to something bigger than our own self-interest.

But when we stay true to our purpose, and discipline ourselves to stay focused, amazing things can happen. In the heart of Milan, a fortress, the Sforza Castle, was built during the Renaissance. It is now a series of marvelous museums. One has Roman artifacts and ruins, another has musical instruments from the eleventh and twelfth centuries, and then there's one small museum, which has only one statue in it—the last statue the great Michelangelo ever carved, called the Rondanini Pieta. Michelangelo started work on this statue in 1552. It's unfinished, but it's still a remarkable image of Mary holding Jesus when he came off the cross. The faces of Mary and Jesus are magnificent. My daughter, Molly, had spent the last year and a half attending school in Milan and when Claudia and I visited her in 2016, I took the opportunity to see this beautiful statue. When I saw it, I sat there mesmerized for well over twenty minutes. Later, I learned that Michelangelo was working on the statue two days before he died. He was eighty-eight years old.

Michelangelo, of course, is one of the greatest painters and sculptors in the world. However, I love to tell this final story of him because it tells us something significant about the power of purpose. Michelangelo died in 1564, when the average age of an Italian man was probably under thirty. Michelangelo ate the same food, drank the same water and wine as other Italians; there was no special elixir he was taking, no antibiotics to take to combat rampant sickness and disease. There are also stories of the pain that Michelangelo endured while painting the Sistine Chapel in the Vatican, often on his back for long periods of time.

What allowed this man to live almost three times as long as others? The only explanation I can discern of why he lived so long was that he had an amazing sense of purpose. He lived to create—to paint and sculpt. I believe his sense of purpose was so energizing, it gave him his will to live and even at the age of eighty-eight, to keep carving away at another remarkable stone masterpiece.

It's very easy to lose sight of our bigger purpose. We must cultivate the discipline that lets us stay true to our purpose and reason for being. How can we remind ourselves throughout the day? How can we focus and keep our attention on it? For Randall Jones, it's writing it on the whiteboard in his office, remembering he's the water carrier and joyfully connecting the service to his bigger purpose. Whatever you do, help yourself have a magnificent life by ensuring you have great clarity of purpose and then create pathways and habits that allow you to reflect on and move toward that purpose as frequently as possible.

For me, it's going through my morning ritual of reflecting on my six Ps. When it's teaching, I remind myself that while people will forget what I tell them, they'll remember how I made them feel, and if I can inspire them, it's easier for them to learn something new that hopefully will help them lead more effective and remarkable lives. When it's coaching, my purpose is to create an authentic connection with my clients and through that connection, help them gain new insights that will help them be more effective and successful in their lives. I also try to support their efforts to move those insights to commitments to actions and ultimately new results. While it now only takes moments to review and reflect on my big purpose when teaching or coaching, the habit keeps me grounded and centered on how I can best serve and support others and it keeps me happy, satisfied, and fulfilled.

Several years ago, I spoke at my church about the life of Alice Herz-Sommer. In February 2014, she died at the great age of 110! At that time, Alice was the world's oldest survivor of the Holocaust. She was imprisoned at Theresienstadt, which was conceived by Hitler as a "model" concentration camp. Can you imagine the horrors and suffering she witnessed? Alice was a pianist, and in between the summer of 1943 and the camp's liberation at the end of the war, she played more than 100 concerts as a prisoner at Theresienstadt. Most were solo recitals culled from memory from her extensive repertoire.

In the camp, Alice found the kind of meaning that Viktor Frankl spoke of as she learned what she could live without. *Rather than grieving for what she did not have, she rejoiced in what she had.* Alice knew that no one could rob her of the treasures of her mind. "I am richer than the world's richest person because I have music in my heart and mind," she said at the age of 108. While performing, she and the other performers could nearly forget their hunger and their surroundings. Besides the terror of finding their names on a deportation list for Auschwitz, the fear of dying of starvation, typhus, and other diseases had become a reality. Alice remembers, "As our situation became even more difficult, we tried even harder to reach for perfection, for the meaning in the music. Music was our way of remembering our inner selves, our values and our spirit. Music was our food, our religion and our hope," she says. "Music was life. We did not, could not, and would not give up." I think we can all use the wonderful life of Alice Herz-Sommer as someone who found meaning and purpose in her life through music and it was indeed a springboard into enormous happiness, joy, and well-being.

This notion of purpose is not rocket science. Nor is it a new discovery. It's been with us a long, long time. Yet, so many people go to their graves never having gotten clear about their purpose. When you have a mighty purpose, it can sustain you through all sorts of difficulties and challenges. When you have a purpose, a big, mighty purpose, you live longer, you're happier, and you're healthier.

Viktor Frankl created logotherapy, which is the realization that a life well-lived has a deeper sense of purpose and meaning. When we talk about happiness, we're not talking about pleasure because pleasure is fleeting. If I have $10, and I give you that $10, I no longer have that money. But if I give you my love and admiration, the more I have and the more I gain in return. Meaning is like that. When you live a life with deep meaning and purpose, the more you give away, the more you have.

REFLECTION AND ACTION

Before you move on to the next chapter, please consider reflecting on and writing down your responses to the following questions related to "Living with Purpose":

When do you feel most alive?

....

....

What are those activities that give you great meaning and joy in your life?

....

....

What is your life calling you to be or do on this earth?

....

....

What is or will be your legacy? What do you want to most be remembered for?

....

....

Write the first description that comes to mind to complete this sentence: *Looking back, my life's purpose was to:*

....

....

Based upon your answers to the questions above, how would you define your life's purpose today?

....

....

How can you keep this purpose in front of you over the next several weeks and months so that it is helping you stay true, focused, aligned and energized?

....

....

Chapter 6

CULTIVATING OUR POSITIVE EMOTIONS

All good doctors are trained to hunt for the bad, to find illness or things that need to be operated on, removed, or cut. That was true of Dr. Mike Dietz, who was trained as a surgeon and is now a hospital administrative leader where he is responsible for overseeing a demanding service line of physician specialists at a very large health system on the East Coast. In fact, Dietz was especially good at hunting for the bad, and this made him an especially good physician and surgeon. Dietz's problem, though, was that he carried that hunting for the bad into the majority of his interactions and relationships. His otherwise useful pessimistic view of the world wasn't just a part of him at work, but throughout the rest of his life. He was often searching for what was wrong, what needed to be fixed and resolved, and sure enough, he found plenty of it all around him. And when you constantly are trying to fix things and people, it often puts an enormous strain on one's relationships. That was certainly the case for Mike.

I shared with him about the importance of learning how to hunt for the good, a well-established tool in resiliency. It resonated with him. He knew he hunted for the bad, and now he had to learn how to be as good at hunting for the good.

Essentially, hunting for the good is as simple as making sure that we are looking for positive things that we or others are doing or are involved in that we could notice and affirm. Martin Seligman was also a pioneer in identifying hunting for the good as a key skill in improving one's resiliency.

To help himself, Dr. Dietz took a journal with blank pages and labeled the front with a sticker that said, "The Good Book." In the book, he deliberately made daily entries about the good things that he observed that day. That was the discipline to get him to change his mindset. And as he showed me his "good book," there was a big smile on his face and an excitement about the practice that he was proud of. He reflected that by going through the intentional process of keeping track of the good stuff, he could see it making a more positive difference in his relationships with others and even with himself.

SOME HUNTING TOOLS

If you don't want to keep a "good book" as Dr. Dietz does, there are now wonderful smart phone apps that can work just as well. I shared previously that I use the app, Gratitude365, which lets me either take a picture or pull a picture from my phone that I consider memorable for the day. It also allows me to make as many entries as I desire to track the positive things that happened in my day. We'll discuss the use of this app further in the chapter dedicated to the habit of gratitude, but the short version is that when I reflect on things that I am grateful for, I am also cultivating positive emotions. And I find making entries each day on my iPhone easy, but remarkably meaningful. As I wrote this chapter, I made three entries for today, and noticed that I have gone 467 straight days in making 1,681 positive entries of things in my life that I am most grateful for.

Another great benefit of having a smart phone is that it allows us to store and quickly access photos. I have found that there are certain pictures that always make me feel happier, more joyful, and positive. We all have those pictures that when you see them, it causes us to momentarily relive the positive memory and experience. I strongly encourage clients to consider during particularly stressful and demanding days, to take several "positivity" breaks to either access a picture that brings them joy or to reflect on a happy experience they had, or even to reflect on an upcoming event they are eagerly looking forward to.

Another app I use now is called MoodKit. It has all sorts of activities that research says will bring you enjoyment and cultivate positive emotions if you do them. One activity is to write down three of your life dreams and picture yourself having achieved them. For me, one of my dreams is to be around when my granddaughter, Estelle, gets married. (She's two and a half, I'm fifty-eight—so it is a great motivator to stay healthy and positive, so that I can live as long as possible.) Another activity is to write down what you appreciate about your life. This counters all the negative that we constantly see, in the news and in our lives.

For Dr. Dietz, keeping his "Good Book" has been helping him be and stay more positive, and by cultivating more positive emotions, it is improving the quality of his key relationships. By writing down the good, he's not only able to recognize and appreciate all the good in his life and express that appreciation to others, but he's also better able to fix what's broken, as he can approach problems and difficulties with greater positive emotion. Celebrating the good has even positively impacted his non-work relationships. He has a wife and two daughters who have benefited greatly from his balance of the positive and negative.

REWIRING FOR THE GOOD

As I have had the opportunity over the last several years to share with audiences my insights around joy, happiness, resiliency, and well-being, I share some of my military experiences and talk about why it's so important for soldiers to be able to hunt for the good. Imagine a soldier who has seen combat, who is trained to and used to hunting for the bad—that's how he's managed to survive on the battlefield—and who goes home to a spouse and two young children. I have shared before how that soldier's trained hypervigilance has the potential to cause an overreaction to something as innocent as a glass dropping and shattering. If his instincts are wired for the bad, who knows how he might react? He needs to practice not getting angry and letting it go. A broken glass is not worth the cost of a negative interaction with your child, but it's the kind of thing that happens all the time. If that pattern continues long enough, the child will take that nature into his or her own life as well.

I was watching the news just this morning that reported how a young veteran walked into a medical facility focused on treating veterans suffering from PTSD and, after a lengthy hostage situation, took the life of three caregivers before taking his own life. I am sure we will know more of the story over the weeks ahead, but I wonder, if this young soldier could have better cultivated and hunted for the good in his life, if this tragedy might have been averted.

We're hardwired as a species to look for the bad stuff. Our ancestors stayed alive by being hypervigilant to any threat and by being aware of everything that could go wrong. It's our natural instinct and we have to recognize that always being hypervigilant and overly anxious can be lethal to ourselves and others.

One of my closest friends, Michael Montelongo, knows a lot about world events and politics. Like me, he's also a graduate of Harvard Business School and West Point. While Michael once held the prestigious role of Chief Financial Officer of the Air Force, overseeing a budget of well over $80 billion, he and I also spent many weekends together serving young adults, prisoners, and even young soldiers in religious retreats. Michael and I are aligned on so many issues involving politics and religion. Yet, only several months ago, we got into a very contentious argument about healthcare. And I am not proud of how I let my emotions get away from me as I no longer focused on understanding his different perspective but instead focused on trying to win our argument so I could be right and affirm that he was wrong.

However, at some point in our heated disagreement, I

realized that I was emotionally getting out of control and becoming less thoughtful and articulate in not only making my case but in fully appreciating my dear friend's perspective and point of view. I was so grateful of my awareness to step back from the argument, because I know that many times in my past, I was unable to recognize being out of control and just stayed in the argument until it ended in an emotional mess that then often required massive amounts of humility and recovery to get the relationship back on track.

I make this point because we often don't realize how easily we can be pulled into negative emotions and for us to become defensive and focus on the bad. When I'm at my best, one of my strengths is communication and connection. But when I'm pulled into negative emotion, my capacity to think critically diminishes and it becomes markedly more challenging to promote trust and mutual respect, listen, connect, affirm, and relate to others. Positive emotion on the other hand is the gateway to effective relationships that includes working more effectively in teams, coaching others toward improvement, finding new, innovative approaches to seemingly intractable problems, or just taking the time to listen to a colleague vent or share something challenging in their lives.

As we have discussed before, physically, in the heightened state of fear and the amygdala hijack, the body decreases blood flow to the prefrontal cortex and sends more to our limbs so we can fight or flee. The more we see into the brain and into the body, the more we see how good cultivating positive emotion is for us and just how negative emotion can adversely affect the quality of our lives. When people have prolonged stress, it's debilitating mentally, physically, and emotionally.

We simply need to train ourselves to be as keenly wired for positive emotion as we are for negative emotion. And we need to be intentional about it. We need to adopt habits to keep us on track, like Dr. Dietz does with his "Good Book."

BROADEN AND BUILD POSITIVITY

Focusing on positive emotions doesn't just affect us. We can also use it to impact others—which often can come back and positively impact ourselves. There's a theory I like, known as "broaden and build." When we're around people who are positive and enthusiastic, it's hard not to be impacted by that. Southwest Airlines is great at customer service. I used to show a video of a flight attendant rapping the safety talk. Imagine being on that plane. Most passengers aren't overly joyful to be traveling, packed like sardines into the plane, having to go through security, and then there's always that annoying speech the flight attendants have to give about safety. The flight attendants probably get tired of giving it, and most passengers don't want to hear it. And usually, that's how we experience it, just one more negative thing throughout the day. But this Southwest video is wonderful because it shows how a flight attendant decided to have some fun with his job. He gets the passengers clapping and nodding along. Almost instantly, the passengers started smiling and laughing. It wasn't much effort on the part of the flight attendant—in fact, doing something fun probably felt like less effort than just giving the same old speech. It didn't take any more time for the flight attendant to do this, either. He just decided to approach a situation with positivity, and he allowed that positivity to spread. Imagine being on that plane. Imagine the different state you would be in once you were on the runway, and how that would impact the rest of your flight. Now imagine being the flight attendant. It's your fifth flight of the day. Are you bored and slogging through it, or are you taking more joy in your work?

I fly just about every week, usually on Delta Airlines as I live in Atlanta, Delta's hub. Several weeks ago, on one of my flights, the pilot came out of the cockpit and started walking down the aisle introducing himself as the captain, thanking the passengers for flying Delta and being as positive as possible in engaging us. I watched the passenger reactions and it was amazing how they and I quickly shifted our attitudes toward the positive.

That experience reminded me of another recent experience that makes this point with even greater poignancy. Recently, I was meeting a friend, Danny, at a restaurant in downtown Atlanta for lunch. As we were at a table waiting for our food to be delivered, we were surprised when the waitress who brought the food told us that in addition to our food, we were entitled each to a hug. Danny and I both took our turns as this kind woman gave each of us a warm embrace. The woman's name was Lydia and it was clear that she loved her job. While HR policies might frown upon Lydia's extra service, the impact of Lydia's hugs on Danny and I was palpable. As we were getting up to leave, a woman asked if she could have our table. We said yes but also told her about taking advantage of Lydia's hugs and the woman indicated that she often comes to the restaurant specifically for Lydia's hugs and refers to her as the "Angel of the Restaurant."

There's a picture I've always shared with clients, explaining how I access positive emotions. I shared in a previous chapter that one of the happiest experiences of my life was in taking Claudia to St. Lucia for our twenty-fifth wedding anniversary. The picture I keep and reflect on is of Claudia and I next to each other under a canopy behind our dinner table on the beach with two Tiki torches burning brightly. We are both smiling deeply and extraordinarily happy. I love to tell the story, too, because every time I tell it, it takes me back to the experience and it will always be a source of happiness, joy, and positive emotion for me.

When I share it, it's also a source of positive emotion for my clients because they get impacted by my positive emotion. Once again, the upward spiral. Broaden and build.

When you are having a difficult day, why not pull out a picture that quickly connects you with a memory of joy and happiness? While it perhaps cannot change the demands of your particular situation, it can change how you view that situation. We can do this any time, even if it isn't easy. In fact, it's during the tougher times, when we're feeling negative, that it's most important to remember to access our positive emotions. That's when we need to train ourselves to keep perspective. That's when having those pictures or keeping track of the good in our lives can come in handy. One look at a picture of your spouse, your kids, a great vacation, or peak experience can spark more positive emotion that in turn can shift your attitude, disposition, and ultimately your interactions with others.

To remind myself of this, I always return to what Viktor Frankl showed us, that even in the midst of deep, dark despair, we can find happiness. "The last of one's freedoms is to choose one's attitude in any given circumstance." I continue to believe this may be one of the most transformative ideas in the world—that we do not have to wait for the world to accommodate our needs. Instead, we can change our attitude. We can act and react differently to what life throws at us and choose happiness, joy, and resiliency instead. I will forever be thankful that Frankl did not take his life and instead shared that through his imaginary conversations with his wife while being forced to march to brutal work camps, he discovered the transformative power of love. If he could do it in a concentration camp, I know I can certainly do it when I spill my coffee on my pants or when my friend starts talking politics.

THE IMPORTANCE OF PERSPECTIVE

Daniel Gilbert, a prominent sociologist at Harvard, wrote a very interesting and provocative book, *Stumbling on Happiness*. His book is about how what we think leads to happiness isn't often the case and that we often miss what actually does lead to happiness. Again, there is that misconception that accomplishing things or being rich will equal happiness. But what's true is that whatever happiness set point we had before, say, winning a lottery, may spike up for a while, but it will eventually go back to that set point. (In fact, in many cases, a lottery winner's life actually gets worse.) Gilbert says the best vacations are the ones that have the most meaningful experiences associated with them and that includes things that "didn't go accordingly to plan." Those experiences—not necessarily the most expensive or extravagant ones—are the vacations you continue to reflect on because they were interesting, extraordinary, and certainly memorable.

I can attest to this. Claudia and I went on vacation several years ago with our close friends, Peter and Sarah, to Morocco and Spain. Claudia and Sarah thought it would be a great idea for us to go south from Marrakesh in Morocco by van and then take a camel ride into the Sahara Desert where we could stay in a desert camp and sleep under the stars. With not much reflection, I thought it sounded interesting and certainly different and I didn't think about it much beyond that. I was also busy at the time with some key work projects and I had not paid much attention to all the elements of the itinerary for this grand idea.

It turned out to be an eight-hour trip from Marrakesh to the Sahara Desert by van over one of the most treacherous roads in the world over the High Atlas Mountains. The van driver, Hassan, apparently didn't like air conditioning, so we sat in his sweltering van on a hot day in the desert while he raced over the dangerous terrain, terrifying us as he sped around curves without guard rails. We would ask him to put on the air conditioner and he would do so for only a few minutes before turning it off again. Regrettably, I was sitting up front and experienced car sickness as we swerved through each switchback.

Once we finally arrived in a little town on the outskirts of the Sahara Desert, we began a two-and-a-half-hour camel ride. Suddenly, having just survived the eight-hour ride with our driver, still feeling carsick, riding on a camel didn't seem so romantic. If you've never been on a camel, I would suggest the fifteen-minute ride rather than the several-hour version. It was incredibly bumpy and certainly not conducive to a man's anatomy when riding it like a horse. Camels, also, are not the cleanest animals around. And think about the scenes of a desert. Not a lot of changing landscapes or colors. My dear friend Peter's camel, believe it or not, was named "Maurice" and we are to this day convinced that Maurice had some serious issues, and the foam coming out of his mouth or the tantrums he threw intermittently while Peter was riding him, were all part of his demented pathology.

At the time, it was quite easy to complain about some of the minor hardships of our journey. Finally, we arrived at a little camp where our guides had set up a wonderful dinner feast for us to enjoy on the desert floor. The plan was to sleep on the sand—and that was when we looked to the sky.

There are no lights in the desert, nothing to drown out the magnificence of the night sky—and that was what it was, simply magnificent. It was astounding, breathtaking. A completely open sky just bursting with stars—and then just us, there on the sand.

What is most remarkable is that my friends and I have retold our journey to the desert story, dozens of times, and it always gives us immense joy in retelling the story. And the things we complained about then are things we regale now. And I cannot begin to tell you how much laughter we have enjoyed in talking about Peter's camel, Maurice, or in describing our van driver, Hassan.

Telling this story brings us continued, immense joy—not in spite of the things that went wrong, but, in part, because of them. Adversity, strange as it seems, can be a powerful tool in accessing positive emotions.

Work to cultivate positive experiences in your life, the ones that will allow you to tell and retell the experiences over and over with great joy and laughter.

RIDING YOUR HORSE

One of my favorite clients is a neurosurgeon and Chief Medical Officer. His name is Don Kendrick. We had developed a wonderful coaching relationship, and then he invited me to speak at a physician retreat that he organized where I spoke on resiliency and physician burnout avoidance. After a very successful retreat, he invited me to his home in Alabama where we fished, and Don drove me around his beautiful 280-acre ranch. While giving me the tour, he stopped his truck by a horse. You could tell through Don's emotions that he clearly had a strong connection to the animal. Dr. Kendrick warmly and softly spoke of his horse, "That horse and I have won many trophies. He's one of my dearest friends. I haven't ridden him in a year and I really miss that."

That night, I told him: "You should ride your horse."

The next day after I had flown back home, he sent me a text with a picture of himself on his horse. He wrote: "Here I am in my happy place." Don had given me—and himself—a wonderful gift.

Most of us have that happy place—our own version of the horse we should be riding. We simply need to identify what gives us positive emotion and then carve out time to do those things. One of my goals is to play piano for sixty minutes each week and sing for thirty minutes. That is my happy place. Writing this book has turned out to be more challenging than I thought it would be and last weekend, I deliberately focused on getting as much done on the book as possible while recognizing that other important things in my life would be delayed. However, I realized that before the weekend was out, I just needed to get several minutes back on my baby grand piano and belt out a few songs. I was really glad I did. I sang a few songs and it was wonderful medicine.

Sometimes, it feels like our happy place should just present itself to us, but the truth is we must be intentional. It has to be a priority like anything else.

I love this beautiful quote from the poet and author Mary Oliver: "Tell me, what is it you plan to do with your one wild and precious life?"

If you could design your life, wouldn't you design it with more joy, happiness, and significance? A few days ago, I was with a client who lost a loved one completely unexpectedly, and with another client who shared that they suffered a heart attack many years earlier and that it was a wake-up call to not let the little annoyances get in the way of paying attention to what was most important. We are not promised tomorrow. Each of us has no idea how long we have on this wonderful planet and because of that, why not make this one wild and precious life as incredible as possible!

We must figure out how to not let life live us, but how we can live life. It's about living our lives with great intention. We should be intentional about cultivating and savoring positive emotions and experiences. We need to be crystal clear about what gives us great happiness and then intentional about filling each day, week, month, and year with those things.

REFLECTION AND ACTION

Before you move on to the next chapter, please consider reflecting on and writing down your responses to the following questions and activities related to "Cultivating Our Positive Emotions."

Charting our Positive Experiences: Please reflect on at least three to five positive experiences that you had either today or yesterday:

....

....

....

....

....

How might you incorporate this reflection exercise into your daily life?

....

Please watch the short video at: https://youtu.be/ Cgw8OFVHzd4. What would it be like to start your day with such positive emotion and affirmation as this precious little girl? What three affirmations could you write that would help you stay as positive as possible today?

Affirmation 1: ....

Affirmation 2: ....

Affirmation 3: ....

How might you make affirmations a part of your daily rituals?

....

Happy Days: The practice of remembering happy life events and attempting to replay them in one's mind to prolong and reinforce positive emotions. List at least three of your happiest moments over the last several years.

Memory 1: ....

Memory 2: ....

Memory 3: ....

How might you keep these happy moments and memories at your fingertips so that when you are having a frustrating or overwhelming day, you can draw upon these happy memories to bring you moments of joy, happiness, and positive emotion?

Creating a Savoring Album: Most of us now have smartphones with access to thousands of pictures. If you could create a "savoring album" filled with pictures that when seen, evoke positive emotions and great fun, adventures, momentous occasions, and exciting journeys, what three pictures would you pick?

....

....

....

What could you do to have these pictures put in a prominent or accessible place so that as you go through your day, they might provide you with small pockets of positive emotion as you quickly reflect on the memory?

....

Chapter 7

DEEPENING OUR SOCIAL BONDS

A senior executive I work with named Bob confided in me that his only friend had been his spouse. It's not because he wasn't likeable. It was because all his time was spent serving his family or his career. There simply was no time left over for him to nurture any friendships outside of his immediate family.

This was taking its toll. He was feeling the burden of his job, and he was socially isolated. He told me one of the saddest things I've heard: "I have no friends." Yet, very quickly it took me back to my dear friend and social worker, Kempton Haynes, who after our fourth session, told me, "Man, I would hate to be your wife." I could deeply relate to my client's situation. It seems that it's not that uncommon. Too many of us focus on professional success and accumulation at the expense of building deep, intimate relationships with others.

Too often, this is much more so the case for men. Ever hear of a book club for men? I know they exist, but it just is not that common. I recall being asked at church many years ago if I would be interested in joining a men's group. I excitedly said yes. When I went to the first meeting, the host asked everyone what movie we wanted to watch as he had a large home theater he was quite proud of, and what type of pizza we would like. The dominant movie choice was an "action" movie. While I was expecting an opportunity to deepen my understanding of the men in the group to include building sufficient trust so that I also could open up and share myself, watching a movie in a dark home theater obviously did not facilitate that. After the movie, the group broke up and I didn't return.

I asked my client, Bob, to reexamine his purpose. His original purpose was to be a successful business leader and aspire to the highest levels of corporate leadership. He had arrived, and yet found the destination less than fulfilling. I asked him to consider shifting his view from success to significance. I think they are very different. Success refers to the level of accomplishment; significance refers to the quality of the impact of that success on others. I asked him, "How can you play a bigger role in lifting others up and perhaps even passing on your immense talents to others? And as part of that, how can you form deeper connections and expand your social network?"

As he began to challenge himself toward a life of greater significance, he started reinvesting his time and energy into some of his old networks. Bob graduated from West Point and started reaching out to alumni where he lived. He started organizing gatherings and was a catalyst for other alumni to deepen their bonds. As we have also spent more time together, it has been wonderful watching my friend be happier and more fulfilled.

He is now delighted with this new chapter of his life. It's no longer about success but about having people besides your spouse or children to share it with. We all need a rich social network of people who care about us, who enjoy time with us, and who we enjoy time with. (I just received a text from him as he is trying to put together another social event!)

Remember Buettner's book *The Blue Zones*? On Buettner's website, you can take a free eLearning course about what Buettner calls the "Power Nine": the nine things that are common in all of the blue zones. Of the nine, three have to do with high-quality relationships: 1) Having a loving, nurturing, close-knit family. 2) Beyond the family, having a tight circle of friends that you enjoy spending time with. These friends are the ones you can call at 2 a.m. and they would drop everything and come running. 3) Feeling a strong sense of belonging to a community. Faith communities are most common, but it doesn't have to be affiliated with a church. Maybe you actively belong to the Rotary Club or Chamber of Commerce or you live in a small town where "everyone knows your name."

OVERLOOKING SOCIAL BONDS

So why do we avoid close and intimate relationships? It's the way we're wired for survival. Self-protection says, "Never let people see who you really are. Never let them know you're deeply insecure or afraid, or overly anxious." There's nothing scarier than being intimately vulnerable. Just recently, I facilitated a client strategic retreat and over lunch had the leaders share their answers to this question: "What has been one of the hardest things you have had to overcome in your life and has shaped who you are today?" When I cued up the question, several leaders verbally groaned, and I could see a few eye rolls as well, indicating to me that for some of the leaders, sharing themselves was not something they wanted to do or would enjoy doing.

As a faculty member at West Point, I saw in the majority of my male students a need to prove their masculinity. (My female students were also wired to prove themselves, but I sensed it was a different developmental focus for them and frankly found them to be more emotionally mature.)

Every cadet has to be an athlete, put on a helmet, be a warrior, and carry a weapon, so it's the perfect place to prove yourself. But it doesn't do much to cultivate your softness, to open up your heart to be intimate with another person. As a young cadet, I don't recall being told that a key leadership tool would be listening with empathy. I am not sure I even heard the word empathy ever mentioned by anyone because I was probably not listening. I am grateful that my own personal journey has shown me that one of the best things I can do for another person is to listen to them with empathy and appreciation.

In the early days of my company, leadership*Forward*, one of my first healthcare clients was Larry, who worked as a senior executive at the Deaconess Billings Clinic in Billings, Montana. We've become good friends over the years. I had been brought in to help his senior leadership team develop better cohesion and alignment with each other. In order to deepen the trust amongst the team members, it was important to ask the leaders to be more vulnerable. To do that, I asked each team member to share a significant experience in their life that helped shape who they were as leaders.

When it was Larry's turn, he shared how he had been diagnosed with ulcerative colitis while in medical school at Stanford. Ulcerative colitis can be a debilitating and difficult disease to control and manage. He shared that as he dealt with the disease, he would go through these cycles of weight loss, trying to regain it and then losing it again as he dealt with many complications related to the disease, all while trying to get through the demanding experience of medical school.

As Larry was sharing his story, he became emotional. He choked up as he described the two "angels" in his life, his mom and his fiancé, who supported him in so many ways during his struggle. Because of them, he got through medical school and realized his dream of becoming a physician.

To put people at ease over the emotion Larry was showing, I said, "A lot of you have been working with Larry for many years. I'm sure you've heard this story well before now and I apologize for having Larry retell such an emotional experience."

Yet, to my great surprise, no one had. He'd never told it, despite many of the team having known Larry for several years. The organization's Chief Nursing Officer followed Larry and she, too, emotionally shared some extraordinary lessons in courage, failure, and difficulty. And once again, I apologized for having a team member share some painful experiences that I was sure the team had heard before. And again, no one on the team had heard the stories.

That's been my experience since then, too. So many of the

stories of who we really are, we never tell. Rarely do we ask, and rarely do we share. And I have come to love and welcome people's stories because when we really know each other's stories, we get to see each other in deeper and more intimate ways. After Larry told his story about dealing with his disease and the help he got from his fiancé (who would later become his wife), I could never see Larry in the same way again. I now held a deep respect for his passion and determination to overcome difficulties and challenges.

When we know each other's stories, we connect to each other in deeper ways. I shared previously about the client who shared that when he was thirty-nine, he suffered a heart attack, and that changed how he has lived his life ever since to include not letting insignificant things get him excited or concerned. Now that I have that understanding and appreciation of his experience, I know I will relate to him in very different ways.

When I speak with clients, I have gotten more comfortable telling my stories to include how I suffered from deep insecurities. And instead of it pushing other people away, I have found that often the deep truths of our lives connect us and allow us to relate to people in more meaningful and authentic ways.

While the seven habits I discuss in this book are all important, I have come to believe that deepening our social bonds with others may be the most important for us to nurture. As Americans, we hold dear this mythology of the rugged, isolated individual who through the sweat of his brow and the strength of his back, our country was won. We place so much emphasis on individual rights. Even the movies we watched as kids had protagonists overcoming extreme odds—John Wayne, Rocky, etc. The idea of being alone and taking on the world is almost romanticized. And we actually enacted laws such as the Homestead Act of 1862, where anyone could be granted 160 acres of public land in exchange for a small filing fee and 5 years of continuous residence on the land. This contributed significantly to the westward expansion of America but also created tremendous distance between people. In Europe, farmlands encircled villages and at the end of each day, farmers would leave their fields to go back to their village and gather with family and friends. If you owned several plots of 160 acres, that was much harder to do. If you needed to borrow a cup of sugar, it was quite an ordeal. The notion of the rugged, triumphant individual still prospers greatly to this day and it can be a cultural and psychological barrier to seeing the successful life as a collective and collaborative effort.

If we are honest about history and our own experience, nothing really significant in life ever gets accomplished by just one person. An author writes and a piano player plays, but there are scores of others who encouraged them to make it happen. Someone paid for the piano lessons and made sure they practiced every day. Someone read, critiqued, and published the writer's work. Someone taught them. Someone listened. Parents, siblings, friends, spouses, and colleagues all make the magic happen for dreams to be accomplished.

Harvard University has conducted the longest study on adult development. They started with 724 young men beginning in 1938 and studied them physically, psychologically, behaviorally, and socially every year since then. While there are just a few of the remaining men alive, the study continues as the longest longitudinal study of adult development ever conducted. The clearest lesson from this study is that *great relationships keep us happier and healthier,* and it's the quality of our close relationships that matter most, not fame, wealth, education, or high achievement.

Beyond the Harvard Study, the research keeps piling up that building close, intimate relationships is essential to a wonderful life and yet, many of us are not taught that when we're young, and the resulting idea that we must go it alone persists into adulthood. But as Bob and others have shown us, it's never too late.

STRENGTH IN NUMBERS

As I shared earlier in the book, I had a blast attending the Army retirement of my dear friend, Dan York. I now know at this point in my life it was important that I show up for the retirement to connect and bond with someone I have such deep respect for and to see some of our mutual friends. It isn't something I would have done even fifteen years ago. When I was a young cadet at West Point, I spent the majority of my time trying to figure out how to get the top prizes in academics and leadership, not on building deep, enduring friendships. But now—armed with research, intention, and discipline—I try to make up for lost time and nurture friendships that will last with people I respect and care deeply about. I know it's good for me, and hopefully my friends and family benefit as well from my engagement and desire to grow closer. It helps me be the best coach, teacher, dad, and husband I can be. It's not a luxury. It's a priority.

Lonely people are markedly less healthy than sociable people. Happy people have richer social networks, and social connectedness also contributes to a lack of disability as we age.

In Sebastian Junger's book, *Tribe: Homecoming and Belonging*, he suggests some of the prolonged post-traumatic stress of soldiers returning from war is not because of the horrors they experienced on the battlefield but because when they came back home, they entered a life of extreme isolation in sharp contrast to the intimacy and deep human bonds they had developed with their comrades in battle. According to a report published by the VA in 2016, which analyzed 55 million veterans' records from 1979 to 2015, an average of 20 veterans a day take their lives. What a terrible tragedy that these men and women who were willing to sacrifice themselves in service to their country, would take their lives through suicide. I wonder how many of them would not have died if they had learned to open themselves up to help, made themselves vulnerable to trusting others, and were able to replace their deep bonds in combat with deeper bonds in peace.

That's an extreme (yet incredibly important) example, but it's true of all of us. We need to be more conscious of the importance of developing and deepening our social bonds. For whatever reason, it's one of those things we all tend to think we know. Just as many of us who are parents have never read a book on parenting, we likewise don't read books nor are intentional on how to have significant and intimate relationships with others.

BEWARE THE PSEUDO-COMMUNITY

Scott Peck wrote *A Different Drum*, where he made a great distinction between a pseudo-community and a real community. Pseudo-community is where members are extremely pleasant and avoid all disagreement in "making nice" with one another. People, wanting to be loved or unwilling to face hard issues, withhold some of the truth about themselves and their feelings in order to avoid conflict. Individual differences are minimized, unacknowledged, or ignored. The group may appear to be functioning smoothly, but individuality, intimacy, and honesty are minimized for the sake of harmony.

Real community emerges as the group chooses to embrace not only the light, but life's darkness. True community is both joyful and realistic. Members feel safe to speak their deepest truths and share their deepest and most vulnerable parts—and others will simply listen. It's only in the real community where we take off our masks, where we open ourselves up to others, where we are vulnerable, but know that vulnerability will not be exploited but respected and cherished. And in real community, we know that to courageously face the conflict will help the community to grow and heal.

Today, in large part because of social media, pseudo-communities are everywhere. Despite how seemingly connected we feel to others, social media too often isn't real. The tendency, for most people on social media, is to only present the good parts of their lives and if they happen to be honest and share their vulnerabilities, the negative and cruel judgment from anonymous people hiding behind their computers can be crushing. It's a curated existence. It's not good for the person doing it, and it's not good for the person seeing or reading it. All that twisted reality can have a negative effect on our mood and self-image. It's hard to live up to the images of others that are constantly being thrown in your face, and it's impossible to live up to the image you present online all the time. It creates this deep psychological disconnect between who you're trying to present and who you really are.

In fact, in our effort to create bonds through social media, it may actually create deeper isolation. No wonder that some of the founding members of companies like Facebook, Google, and Microsoft who now have young children are on speaking circuits, advocating that parents be incredibly careful and limit the time that their children are exposed to online experiences and content.

THE STEPS OF CREATING BONDS

I hope by now you're convinced of this fact: creating stronger social bonds is crucial to our well-being, happiness, and joy. And even though for many of us it's a forgotten skill or simply not our strong suit, it can be done. Let's look at how, step by step.

First, recognize that close relationships are vitally important to having a remarkable life. By now, I hope you're convinced, but I know it's difficult to accept. We live in a society that praises loners. For some reason, it's seen as weakness to share emotions, need help, or to lean on someone. You absolutely must get over that. Having close relationships does not take away from your hard work, your success, or your ability to be independent. In fact, as we've seen, having close relationships can lead to greater success as well as greater happiness.

Denzel Washington said, "At the end of the day, it's not about what you have or even what you've accomplished. It's about what you've done with those accomplishments. It's about who you've lifted up, who you've made better. It about what you've given back."

You must accept that building deeper, intimate relationships is a vital need, like the rest of the habits in this book. You must have the knowledge that deep, meaningful relationships are quintessential to a life well-lived.

Second, take action. Be intentional about spending your time on what really matters to you. Your calendar should reflect your goals. If you've taken the first step just described, then this step shouldn't be as difficult. If it's important, then it's a priority. It's also something we have to realize won't just happen. There's this common misconception that all friendships are purely organic, that they just happen. But they don't. You have to be intentional.

Find ways of reconnecting with old friends or finding new ones and be deliberate in making that friendship flourish and thrive.

If you are struggling to seek pathways to find and build meaningful friendships, here below are a few ideas to consider. Be creative, be curious, and be intentional in expanding your circle of friends:

- Join programs like Habitat for Humanity in your community and participate in a few home builds.
- Seek out volunteer opportunities for community causes. We live in a part of downtown Atlanta where there are many civic organizations constantly recruiting new members to volunteer for special events.
- Join alumni associations from your high school or college and get involved; use social media to find local alumni and plan gatherings.
- Join sports teams; most communities have soccer, kickball, or softball leagues that are frequently looking for new members.
- Many military units that I have been a part of will conduct reunions. Consider attending.
- If you don't presently belong to a church community, consider finding one and get involved early.
- Sign up for local dance lessons.
- Figure out what business networking opportunities are available in your area.

- Join the local Chamber of Commerce; explore possibilities for volunteering your services.

Third, take stock of how well-equipped you are to build positive relationships. If you never interact with your spouse, for example, you're going to have a tough time nourishing a deep, intimate relationship. Increase your interactions and be intentional about making those interactions more positive. Look in the mirror. Ask yourself, "How often am I pushing people away from me because of my judgment or my need to be right? Is there something else I'm doing that pushes people away or makes them feel unwelcome? How well do I model vulnerability? How well do I actually actively listen to others?"

I have come to see in my life that one of my gifts is in seeing and affirming the gifts that others have. Recently, I was with a client who has an incredible capability to make people feel good, appreciated, and heard in every encounter with them. When I see others with great talents, I call those "superpowers." As we met recently, I decided to pay even more attention to how this gifted individual engages me. I noticed immediately that he frequently smiled and always made gentle eye contact. It wasn't long before this client began to affirm my capabilities and acknowledge the positive contribution I have been in his life. And while I was grateful for his affirmation, I also was greatly impressed by his natural skills at building more meaningful relationships with others. I know I have greatly benefited from his superpowers. It is no surprise that in a short several years, he has been promoted twice and is now one of the most senior leaders of his organization.

I use the acronym HAVE as a framework to help us improve the quality of our relationships.

H is for humility. The pathway to vulnerability is being humble. A relationship needs to be two ways. Both people's needs should be met and by being truly humble, you make yourself less important and by so doing elevate the other person's sense of importance. I think humility is regrettably one of the least appreciated values in society today, and yet when we encounter an authentic human being with great humility, it always positively impacts us.

A is for acceptance. It's hard to feel accepted when you're in a relationship with someone who's always judging you. When we are in the presence of someone who really sees and appreciates us for who we really are, we feel safe and are trusting. This creates the conditions for the other person to also feel safe and trustful.

V is for vulnerability. Open up. It's not just healthy for you but will also make others around you feel more welcome and thankful that they know you. Often, people will ask me how I am doing, and I try to have an authentic answer that reflects things I may be struggling with or am challenged by. When we are vulnerable with others, the tendency is for others to be vulnerable with us. I have found that when two people can get in sync with one another through shared vulnerability, they naturally pull together.

I'm still incredulous at times that I make a living having hour-long conversations with a host of people each month. I try not to ever make it about me, but they frequently ask me first, "How are you doing?" because they really care how I'm doing. Our relationship is elevated to a two-way street. They care about what's going on in my life because from the first time we met, I tried to be focused on helping them improve their lives.

Finally, E is for empathy. This is harder for some of us than others. A person doesn't need to be your clone to be your close friend. You can have differences—in fact, you should! Accept those differences. Seek to understand your friends. Empathy is simple but challenging because it requires great effort to put yourself in the shoes and experiences of another. To feel what they feel, hear what they hear, and see what they see. And when we can do that fully, I never cease to be amazed at how rich a relationship can get through this power of empathy.

This isn't necessarily as hard as it sounds. Start with what you know—or, rather, who you know. My friend

Bob reconnected with classmates and friends from West Point, which is what he knew. One thing my wife and I do is buy season tickets to Atlanta's Broadway series, but we buy more than two tickets, always inviting friends to go with us. We also have gatherings at our house several times a month. It's a priority because we know it fills us up and makes our lives incredibly rich.

But sometimes it can be hard. It takes patience and intention. My wife and I decided several months ago to stop going to a church we've been attending for eleven years. It was a great place for us and we developed great friendships and strong social bonds. Yet, four years ago, we moved from the suburbs to the city, and we'd been going back to the suburbs for church. It's thirty-six miles away. Sometimes, it takes hours to get there in bad traffic. We just can't sustain that anymore. We know, though, that we now must build something similar in a new church community. We are actively looking for a church community that can give us the joy, social support, and friendships we've had for the last eleven years.

It's tough, but we are being intentional. We have some work to do to build deeper community relationships where we live now.

It might seem counterintuitive, but service can also transform us. In his book *What Happy People Know*, Dan

Baker tells about when he was medical director at Rancho Mirage, an ultra-spa where the rich and famous go. One of his first clients was a multi-millionaire who was miserable. His kids weren't talking to him, his third wife was asking for a divorce, and his work partners had turned against him.

Dan's first treatment for this man was to have him volunteer on the oncology floor of a children's hospital. It's pretty hard not to be moved by a child suffering from cancer.

These sorts of prescriptions aren't for drugs. They're for experiences that will move your heart and stir your soul. In this case, this man probably focused only on himself and had a knack for alienating others who didn't kowtow to the man's brilliance and capability. He had chosen the pursuit of money and business success over his relationships. Fortunately for him, he realized that his life was in shambles and that if he didn't change how he lived his life, there was a good chance he would die young and miserable, but with a big, unspent bank account being fought over by his angry, detached children. As a volunteer at the children's hospital on the oncology floor, his job was to read stories to children and bring them surprises. His job was to make them smile.

It's pretty hard to get someone else to smile with a frown on your own face. This sort of prescription moves your heart. This man probably had not had his heart moved for a long time, but the experience had a major, life-changing impact on him. Reading about this man in Dan's book reminded me of that beautiful Charles Dickens story, *A Christmas Carol,* where Scrooge has to be haunted by the ghosts of Christmas past, future, and present to shake him to the core, showing him that unless he radically changed how he lived his life to include cultivating greater positive emotion and deepening his social bonds with his family and others, his life was doomed to one of misery and woe. Who has not been moved by watching over Christmas one of the many versions of the story in film, when Scrooge wakes up on Christmas Day to realize he has another chance at building a beautiful life and he gets to work at it? Shouldn't we all get to work to improve the quality of our relationships?

Fr. Tom Devery is another dear friend who has enriched my life in remarkable ways. He is now a pastor of a Catholic parish in Staten Island, New York. He was the one who introduced me to John Bonviaggio and the beautiful Italian community that did prison ministry on Staten Island. Fr. Tom officiated our wedding thirty-seven years ago when Claudia and I married, and I continue to be reminded of his admonition: "Claudia, your job is to love the hell out of Greg; and Greg, your job is to love the hell out of Claudia, and I know she will always have the harder job!" He also frequently says, "One of the hardest journeys each of us will ever take is the twelve inches from your head to your heart." He's referencing the capacity to love and be loved and to build deep, intimate relationships with others. It takes great courage to make that journey of vulnerability, of humility, empathy, and compassion.

Our world needs those more than ever.

One final story about the importance of building deep intimate bonds with others. Last week a dear friend of Claudia and mine, Scott, died in his sleep of a heart attack. He was only sixty. Our former church choir decided to invite some of the choir alumni to join them at Wednesday night's rehearsal, only two days after Scott's death. At the start of the gathering, the choir director got everyone in a large circle, said a prayer, and indicated that a candle would be passed around and when it got to you, it was your opportunity to share a memory of Scott or to share the impact of his life on yours. There were well over fifty people gathered in the circle and the reflections about Scott's life were quite extraordinary. What really impacted me were the number of people who reflected on the marvelous and compassionate ways in which Scott treated them, made them feel loved and special. No one talked about Scott's net worth, or his job title, or the car he drove. Instead, we spoke of the great care that Scott had given so many gathered in this special circle. I left more inspired and committed than ever to live more like

Scott. I would carry on his memory by actively living and sharing his example with others. Thank you, Scott, for showing some of us the way to a remarkable life!

REFLECTION AND ACTION

Before you move on to the next chapter, please consider reflecting on and writing down your responses to the following questions and activities related to "Deepening Our Social Bonds":

Reflecting on those who have greatly impacted us: Think about three people who perhaps you have not maintained good contact with and yet have played a significant part in your life. Write at least one of them a note reflecting on the positive impact they have had on your life. If they live close to you, consider hand delivering the note; if not, send it by snail mail.

1. ....

2. ....

3. ....

Acts of Kindness: Consider extending an act of random or intentional kindness to someone in need. Write down two examples of these acts that you are confident you can carry out over the next several days.

1. ....

2. ....

What would it look like if you were to increase your daily acts of kindness to others?

The research is compelling. Those who have close friends that they can call at two in the morning to share their difficulties and seek help are much more likely to be healthier and happier. Take an inventory of your friendships by reflecting on four categories of friends:

"Must Friends"—These are very close friends who would be willing to drop everything to come to your support.

....

"Trust Friends"—These are friends with whom you enjoy a strong level of mutual trust and respect and who, with some cultivation and effort, could move to "must friends."

....

"Rust Friends"—These are friends who at some point in your life were meaningful and important to you but the closeness has "rusted" a bit. With some investment of time and effort, perhaps these are also friends that could be moved to "trust" and "must."

....

"Just Friends"—These are the friends who are good acquaintances and relatively in positive relationship. Perhaps a review of these friendships could also warrant more cultivation and effort to move them to "trust" or "must" friends.

....

Chapter 8

REFLECTING AND EXPRESSING GRATITUDE

So many of us move through our days, taking so many things for granted. In the bathroom, for example, you can turn on the hot water faucet and get hot water. Hot water! Almost instantly! And it's clean! For many people in the world, this is a luxury. Even the sky—it's a wonder. It's constantly in flux. Rarely, do we look up to see the beauty and uniqueness of clouds. The majority of Americans have jobs and travel to those jobs in personally-owned cars on well-paved roads. Traffic is regulated by traffic lights where the majority of us actually stop. We have access to dozens of places along our journey that offer fast food that is relatively inexpensive. When we get to work, regardless of the outside temperature, our work environments are highly controlled for comfort and provide us with access to clean toilets and clean workplaces.

If that doesn't paint a clear enough picture, then I highly recommend watching Louie Schwartzberg's TEDx Talk on gratitude (easy to find on YouTube). I've watched this video hundreds of times, and it's an excellent reminder of the magnificent world we live in and the beauty that is all around us that we often take for granted. Schwartzberg's specialty is time-elapsed nature photography, and the video in the talk shows flowers blooming and collecting dew, a strawberry ripening, clouds drifting over mountains—things that are happening around us, all the time, without us taking the time to notice, realize, and appreciate them. Too often, we miss these things completely. At the end of the video, they show faces of people from around the world. It always moves my spirit and my heart because it makes me realize the whole point of the film: when you think about the world we live in, the only response is gratitude.

I've talked already about how, for years, I lived with a rat-race mentality, the idea that when I finally had enough money, achievement, or enough stuff I'd be happy. But I now know that if we reflect on what we're grateful for every day, it helps ground us in the present, and it helps us be happy and joyful. The emotional response to gratefulness is one of joy and happiness. Gratitude helps you focus and connect with those positive emotions.

We usually need more discipline to cultivate this habit than the others. There's less tangible "doing" in cultivating gratitude. When we seek to cultivate relationships, for example, we can pick up the phone and call someone. There's a task attached to it. With being grateful, that's less the case. It's more a moment-to-moment thing. While there are tangible steps we can take that help, it's really about cultivating a mindset of seeing the good in things and taking the time to appreciate them—something many of us struggle to do, whether we realize it or not.

It's important for more reasons than you might expect. When we talk about being grateful, there is the obvious—and very important—aspect of it, which is simply being grateful. But, when you're thinking about what you're grateful for, you're *not* thinking about what you're *not grateful* for. The mind can really only do one thing at a time. When you're in a place of gratitude, it's difficult to feel anger, frustration, disappointment, or sadness. The whole focus is to reflect on what's good in life right now. Gratefulness helps happiness become the default mode of the brain.

A CASE STUDY IN GRATITUDE

Let's look at a case study that we explored in Chapter 3 on happiness. My client Linda described herself as "stuck." When she broke down her problems into one word, that's what she came up with. She was in a relationship that was no longer working, in a job where she felt underappreciated and with little opportunities for advancement, and living in a place that no longer felt like home. One of the first things I asked her is what it would look like if she started reflecting on the blessings in her life at the end of each day and to write them down in a gratitude journal. She started doing that and now she calls the habit "life-giving."

As I had shared earlier, Linda chose "Move!" as her theme for the year as she knew that staying stuck was no longer an option and that for her to be fully happy, she needed to move. When we spoke, and she shared her theme, I could sense a big psychological burden had been lifted, and while she still had to face the uncertainty of where and what she would move to, there was now a great certainty about her that she would move and the possibility of what was next was energizing and exciting.

She started a gratitude journal, and that habit helped her claim "move" as her theme for the year. She had some fear of the unknown. Many of us do. Even if our lives aren't full of joy, we at least know what to expect. Her habit of gratitude, though, was a way for her to build up her psychological resources and realize what she had at her disposal—her education, talent, abilities, and great resilience. She's also a wonderful doctor, highly trained as an intensivist focused on taking care of the critically acute patients in hospital ICUs. By developing a habit of gratitude, she reminded herself that she was worthy of having an amazing life.

It has been less than a year ago that Linda declared "Move!" as her theme. Seven months ago, she bought a house with a partner and fellow physician she is deeply in love with. She is in a new role that is challenging and where she is being appreciated and valued. The theme worked. She moved. And being grateful for the good things in her life gave her the courage and psychological strength to move on and away from the things she was not grateful for.

How could developing a daily habit of reflecting on and expressing gratitude impact your life? How could it help you see more clearly all the things that have blessed your life? How could it help you see so many things around us that we too often take for granted and, through that reflection, be so much more appreciative of all that you do have? Let's dig even more deeply into gratitude.

THE SCIENCE OF GRATITUDE

In a series of studies conducted by the Greater Good Science Center, in collaboration with Robert Emmons of the University of California, Davis, and funded by the John Templeton Foundation, it has been consistently found that people who practice gratitude report fewer symptoms of illness, including depression, more optimism and happiness, stronger relationships, more generous behavior, and many other benefits. In their studies, they often have people keep gratitude journals for just three weeks and report results that have been overwhelming. In studies of thousands of people, from ages eight to eighty, they found that people who practice gratitude consistently report a host of benefits:

- Physical
  - Stronger immune systems
  - Less bothered by aches and pains
  - Lower blood pressure
  - Exercise more and take better care of their health
  - Sleep longer and feel more refreshed upon waking
- Psychological
  - Higher levels of positive emotions
  - More alert, alive, and awake
  - More joy and pleasure
  - More optimism and happiness
- Social
  - More helpful, generous, and compassionate
  - More forgiving
  - More outgoing
  - Feel less lonely and isolated

The social benefits are especially significant, because

it shows us that gratitude strengthens relationships because it requires us to see how we've been supported and affirmed by other people.

BECOMING GRATEFUL

As I've already said, this is one of the harder habits to discipline yourself for, but it's also one of the easiest in terms of the steps you can take. Focusing on gratitude has been the least difficult task to convince my clients to do because it's easy and quick. You can do it in less than five minutes. Not only is it easy but, as we've already seen, the benefits are enormous. Given the affirming research of keeping a daily habit of gratitude and the positive benefits to our joy, sense of well-being, and capacity to be present, why wouldn't we work to make this an important habit in our lives? And as we have discussed previously, what the mind looks for, it finds.

One of the easiest ways to make gratitude a daily habit is to start a gratitude journal, as we discussed in Chapter 5. This can be an ink-and-paper journal, or something else entirely. I've talked about the Gratitude365 app before, which is great for those of us who might not be the type to sit and write things down, or those of us who are more visual. In this app, you can either take a picture or use a picture already saved in your phone to reflect on something in your day you're grateful for. The app has a calendar that marks every day you've made an entry with a dot. I like seeing those dots of gratitude for each day of the month I have made entries. They give me a little burst of joy and appreciation for all the many blessings that are poured into and pass through my life. I am very proud that I've made 3 to 5 entries every day for the last 467 days and when I reflect on how full my life is, all I can do is feel grateful.

There's so much to be grateful for when we intentionally look for it. When I was in Utah last year on a biking trip through several magnificent national parks, I used a picture every day of my bike ride to start my gratitude entry. I also include personal best bike rides, watching my grandchildren, beautiful weather, nice dinners, or very positive coaching sessions that I experience. I frequently travel by airplane and I often reflect gratitude when the flights leave and arrive on time. It can be anything, big or small. When my granddaughter was in the hospital with pneumonia, my wife sent me a picture of her before she was discharged. She looked so much better! That picture went on my daily gratitude app entry.

The great thing about using an app or just keeping a journal is that it not only becomes a habit in our morning routine, or lunch break, but permeates the rest of our lives. You're consciously and subconsciously on the lookout for things you're grateful for. You're conditioning your mind to be grateful.

Think of it this way. If you were to ask someone, "When's the last time you saw a yellow Volkswagen?" They'd probably say they have no idea. Over the next few days, though, they would surely notice many yellow Volkswagens—because they were looking for them, whether they realized it or not. That idea was present in their minds. They didn't see them before because their mind wasn't fixed on it. Developing a habit of gratitude is a way to train our minds toward living a life of deep appreciation. When you do that, it becomes a self-fulfilling prophecy.

I can tell you it works. I honestly can't remember the last time I had bad service at a restaurant, or the last time I was mistreated by somebody. Maybe I'm just lucky, but I don't think so. I have to believe it's because of my shift in disposition. The law of attraction says we attract what we give off, and we give off what we attract. It's like the piece of scripture that says, "Seek and you shall find. Knock and the door shall be opened. Ask and it shall be given."

It's a virtuous cycle. The more grateful I am, the more things there are to be grateful for.

Here's something else to try.

In my first year at Harvard Business School, my marketing professor, Tom, was an amazing teacher. Right before Thanksgiving break, he had us do an exercise that was profound. He had a piece of paper titled, "Sources of Power," that listed a host of categories such as education, family, faith, health, experiences, and talents. The exercise asked us to take inventory of all that we had in our lives in terms of tangible and intangible assets at our disposal that we could draw upon.

Even today, I can vividly recall what I listed as my sources of power and even though I was only twenty-nine, I was amazed at the fullness of my life: I had a wonderful, supportive, healthy family; I had graduated at the top of my class at West Point, in turn giving me opportunities to attend Harvard Business School; I had three beautiful and healthy children; I had an extraordinary marriage; I had a strong faith and was actively engaged with two church communities; I was in a profession that I loved and had over the course of my eight years in the Army attended professional development programs for at least twenty months of those eight years; the Army had seen fit to promote me to major ahead of my peers; I had travelled the world, living in Panama, Italy, Okinawa, Germany, Korea, Hawaii, and a host of other US states and had amazing adventures in the process; I was healthy and had reasonable interpersonal and analytical skills and, while feeling like I was an admissions mistake at Harvard, was holding my own at a world-renowned graduate program for business.

I realized when I took that inventory that despite all of my self-doubts and insecurities, my life was incredibly rich. When I encounter clients that perhaps are seeing their glass of life as half full, I pull out that assignment from Professor Tom and have them reflect on their blessings and all that is at their disposal to have a remarkable and wonderful life.

Another incredible exercise I ask clients to do is referred to as the "Gratitude Visit," created by Martin Seligman and used for years in the course he teaches on positive psychology. The exercise is rooted in decades of Seligman's research and he has demonstrated with great veracity, the powerful impact the exercise has had on the well-being and happiness of those who have engaged in the exercise with commitment and sincerity. Seligman takes us through the practice:

> *"Close your eyes. Call up the face of someone still alive who, years ago, did something or said something that changed your life for the better. Someone who you never properly thanked; someone you could meet face-to-face next week. Got a face? Gratitude can make your life happier and more satisfying. When we feel gratitude, we benefit from the pleasant memory of a positive event in our life. Also, when we express our gratitude to others, we strengthen our relationship with them. But sometimes our thank you is said so casually or quickly that it is nearly meaningless. In this exercise...you will have the opportunity to experience*

what it is like to express your gratitude in a thoughtful, purposeful manner.

"Your task is to write a letter of gratitude to this individual and deliver it in person. The letter should be concrete and about three hundred words: be specific about what she did for you and how it affected your life. Let her know what you are doing now, and mention how you often remember what she did. Make it sing! Once you have written the testimonial, call the person and tell her you'd like to visit her, but be vague about the purpose of the meeting; this exercise is much more fun when it is a surprise. When you meet her, take your time reading your letter."

I asked one of my long-standing coaching clients, Drew, to consider using the exercise with someone who had been an extraordinary mentor to Drew many years ago. Drew, even in high school, had a strong entrepreneurial drive and was hired by a man named George who owned two McDonald's franchises. George quickly recognized Drew's drive and talent and took him under his wing, carefully teaching Drew all he knew about how to drive operational excellence and profitability through the McDonald's experience. I still remember years ago Drew sharing with me how George showed him the profit impact of an employee dropping a frozen block of fries; several frozen fries being discarded several times a day could have a significant impact on yearly profitability.

Drew selected George because he had realized that George had greatly impacted his life but was not sure that George really knew of his impact. Drew carefully took the time to write George about the extraordinary impact that he had on his life. When George read the letter, it moved him greatly and he called Drew to thank him for the great gift. It is amazing what being vulnerable and authentic can do to touch people's hearts. George's heart was touched as was his wife's and, of course, Drew's. Several months later, Drew visited George in person and as he was returning from his trip, he called me excited to share the experience of his "Gratitude Visit." He profusely thanked me for suggesting the exercise.

Several years later, George's wife called Drew to share the sad news that George had passed away. She also asked if he would be open to coming to George's funeral to speak about George. She shared with Drew that his letter and subsequent trip to visit them had made such a positive and indelible difference in George's life and they were both deeply grateful for Drew's kindness and thoughtfulness. As Drew was coming back from attending George's funeral, he once again called me up to express his great gratitude for engaging him in the process. As I ended my delightful conversation with Drew with a big smile on my face, I was struck once again by the virtuous cycle that being and expressing gratitude can have on our lives.

So many clients I work with have been touched by this simple exercise, and I challenge anyone reading this to consider doing something similar. Drew didn't know that George had only a few more years to live. Drew didn't know that despite the great success that George had achieved in his life, no one had ever taken the time to share with George how his life had touched and changed theirs. As Drew later shared with me, "This is actually one of the reasons this (the gratitude visit) was so powerful to me. I think we often tell people things while they are ill, but it was a different experience when I told him while he was healthy, bringing me closer while he was ill, but more importantly, I knew that he knew my true, unfiltered feelings on his death bed."

So many of us lose sight of all the things that have been poured into our lives, not just things like clean, running water, but the people—the mentors, role models, family members, someone who was kind to us. We owe it to ourselves to spend at least a few minutes of our day appreciating them.

So, who in your life could use a "Gratitude Visit?"

HOW GRATITUDE TRANSFORMS US

There are critics out there who reject the notions of teaching others to intentionally look for the good and positive.

They will say that some of the world's greatest discoveries, as well as its greatest art, comes from "hunting for the bad." I am not advocating that we ignore the bad because you can't get through life without it; it is deeply ingrained within each of us. Seeking out the good and positive is not going to undo 50,000 years of human evolution. We have inherited and passed on to the next generations tremendous amounts of fear and anxiety. It's impossible for us to ignore the bad. It's a habit we don't have to cultivate because it's been cultivated for us in our DNA for those 50,000 years or so. What we need to do is remind ourselves, despite our hardwiring, of how much there is to be grateful for. The habit of gratitude will not take away all the heartache, fear, and anxiety that the human experience presents us. However, gratitude can help us deal with the suffering that humans inflict on themselves.

Gratitude provides inoculation and protection against life's storms and adversities. It's training of the mind and heart to be more disposed to looking for the good and being in a space of gratitude and appreciation. When you fill your life with gratitude and appreciation, you start to share it with others. It comes more naturally.

I met with a group of high-potential leaders in a leadership program recently, and they shared how much fear was in their organization. They asked me how many of my other clients have been able to drive fear out of their organizations. I shared that my own experience is not all that positive, going back to what my friend Dr. Guthrie said about the natural state of human beings being psychological fear. I told them that a core responsibility of good leaders is to recognize this natural state and be intentional about creating a work environment where people feel safe to say what's on their mind, whether it's sharing dissenting views or providing constructive feedback that will help the organization improve, make better decisions, and address challenging issues.

I broke them into groups of three and had them reflect on the things they were most grateful for and then share it with their colleagues. Research shows that 1:00-2:30 p.m. is a low energy point for most of us each day—and that's when this took place. But it was amazing how the energy in that room increased as they did this exercise. You could see more people smiling and laughing. Their positive emotions were high.

I pushed them to find things they were grateful for beyond their family. I asked them to be creative and specifically find things they were grateful for in working for this organization, their colleagues, and beyond. The more specific you can be, the better, I said. They worked for a non-profit healthcare organization, so they had a very noble mission of providing high-quality and compassionate care to patients. I can't think of a more noble and inspiring vision or mission than that.

It shifted people's consciousness toward looking for the good in their lives.

SPREADING GRATITUDE

Again, the more you give away, the more you have. There's plenty of science and literature that talks about the law of attraction, which I've mentioned, but also the law of expansion, which says the things you put your attention and time to tend to expand. If you focus your time and effort on what's important to you, there's a higher probability it will expand. By focusing your attention on the practice or habit of gratitude, the number of things you're grateful for expands and the more you focus your attention on them.

Whatever emotional state we're in affects those around us. In ancient times, if the tribe or clan rejected you, there was a higher probability of you not surviving. We are wired to fit in and be accepted by our kinsmen. We are wired to be in a relationship with others, and to be keenly aware, even subconsciously, of the emotional states of those around us so that we are prepared and ready should someone move into a fit of rage or other severe negative emotion. And when you are so wired toward protection and survival, it is also quite difficult at the same time to be open, innovative, take risks, challenge the status quo, enjoy a good debate, or seek win-win solutions for everyone's needs to be considered and met.

It should be no surprise then that the highest performing teams are the ones that treat each other with great care and make sure all voices are being heard equally and respectfully. That is why creating a habit of being grateful and expressing gratitude can have such a dramatic improvement on a team's performance. When you're in a place of gratitude, it's hard not to be positive, which affects your interactions and communication with others.

There's an acronym, ARE, that I often use with my clients. It stands for Appreciation, Recognition, and Encouragement and these three things are often some of the most important gifts we can give to another. Regrettably, I also find that they are often the least given by leaders to those that work for them. I have mentioned that I have given more than 1,700 leadership assessments over the last 16 years. The assessment I use has 179 elements that people evaluate other leaders on. "Readily gives praise" is usually one of the lowest scored items for leaders. My encouragement to leaders is to give as much ARE as possible. Of course, it must be sincere, and to make it sincere, the leader has to really look for and pay attention to the good so that they can appreciate, recognize, and encourage the good.

I love to challenge client groups I speak to by asking, "How many employees have you heard of who went to HR to quit or complain because they were sick and tired of all the appreciation, recognition, and encouragement they were receiving from their leadership and peers?" I have asked this question to thousands of people and I am still waiting to hear of even one case.

I am very certain I never will.

We know the real answer is that when high performers leave their employers it is often because of their boss, who too often either does not say much of anything at all to them about their performance or instead finds all the things that are wrong and need to be fixed. Think about the world we would have if every day employees went home to their families filled with ARE. They would pass that on to their children and spouses, who might even pass it on to extended family members and friends.

After all, you can't give what you don't have. This practice is about filling ourselves up with gratitude, so that we are in a place to give it away. What's especially beautiful about gratitude is that the more we have, the more we can give away.

And the more we give away, the more we have. You have to love that virtuous cycle.

When noted neurologist and author Oliver Sacks learned he had terminal cancer at age eighty-two, he didn't spend much time in despair. He was filled with gratitude for the incredible life he had been lucky enough to live. Here is what he wrote in regard to his sense of gratitude:

> "I cannot pretend I am without fear, but my predominant feeling is one of gratitude. I have loved and been loved; I have been given much and I have given something in return; I have read and traveled and thought and written... Above all, I have been a sentient being, a thinking animal, on this beautiful planet, and that in itself has been an enormous privilege and adventure."

REFLECTION AND ACTION

Before you move on to the next chapter, please consider reflecting on and writing down your responses to the following questions related to "Reflecting and Expressing Gratitude":

Reflecting Gratitude Journal: Write down three to five things for which you are currently thankful, from the mundane to the magnificent.

....

....

....

....

....

What would it take to make this a daily habit?

Expressing Gratitude and Appreciation: Think of at least three people to whom you owe a debt of gratitude, and express your appreciation in concrete terms through either a hand-written note or a face-to-face encounter.

....

....

....

What would it take to make this at least a weekly habit?

Taking Perspective: Thinking of those in places far more challenging and in difficult places and spaces in their lives. Reflect for a moment about someone you know or perhaps a news story you read or watched where others were facing extraordinarily difficult, challenging, and even severe conditions or consequences. As you reflect on their difficult circumstances, how can it reframe your own conditions and perhaps provide meaningful perspective for you and increase your gratitude for all that you do have in your life?

Chapter 9

PROMOTING HOPE

This chapter is about more than hope—or at least what we commonly think of as hope. Hope isn't sitting around waiting for the best to happen to us. Rather, hope is attached to our purpose and acting with intention. It's about creating clarity of the future. It's being able to clearly communicate and clearly see a compelling and vivid sense of what's to come, and the sense that what's to come is as good as or better than what you currently have.

As you may have already noticed, all of the habits in this book are intricately linked and overlap, and that is true of hope as well. If you follow these seven habits with some discipline, they will contribute immensely to a life of greater happiness and joy, and they also will strengthen your hope that the future will be even better than the present. You'll develop a confidence that will feed your hope. And a habit of envisioning a clear, compelling, and wonderful future (hope) will actually strengthen your present.

Before I walked into the door of a client organization the other day to provide coaching to a group of executive leaders, I went through a short mental exercise so that I was very clear about what I wanted out of my day by reminding myself of my purpose for each of my coaching sessions, and I also practiced this fifth habit of promoting hope by visualizing after each coaching session how I wanted each of my clients to feel after our time together.

I wanted them to be appreciative, grateful, and clear on the ways they could be more effective and happier. I visualized what a good end of the meeting would be with each of the five executives I was meeting with. This habit is more than being hopeful and optimistic in the sense we typically think of them. It's the discipline of envisioning a very clear, compelling, and successful future. This capacity of visualizing our future may be one of the greatest gifts that each of us possess, but like any gift it must be cultivated, promoted, developed, and used. And because we live in a time when our big brains are getting exhausted, stressed, and overtaxed, it is essential to create a habit of promoting hope. Otherwise, it will be just another good idea instead of a meaningful habit that is actively transforming our lives every time we practice the habit.

What is most amazing is that when I take the time to visualize clearly the outcomes I desire as I did with these client executives, it more often than not turns out as good as or better than I envisioned. And what I continue to find is that the more clearly I describe the future outcomes I desire, the greater the likelihood of those outcomes coming to fruition.

Several months ago, I had a disappointing coaching session with an executive who had received negative feedback on a leadership 360 assessment. We were going over her assessment improvement plan that I thought lacked significant detail and realism and I asked the client: "If you put this improvement plan in place, what will be the positive outcome for you? Describe the target situation as clearly as you can."

My client fumbled through an answer. I realized that I needed to get more specific as well and said, "Picture six months from now. Envision specifically the performance and engagement of your team. Describe how your team is working and interacting to achieve the outcomes you desire. And as you see those outcomes, what will you do and say as their leader to help them realize those outcomes?"

Regrettably, her answers continued to be ambiguous and lacking in detail and as I walked away from the session,

I did not have high confidence that her future would be any better than her current state. In the client leader's 360 assessment, her boss gave her this feedback, "You're much too comfortable with the status quo. You don't have timetables, milestones, or high expectations out in the future for yourself, and if you can't envision what greatness looks like for you, how can those you lead envision it either?"

I define promoting hope as being able to do just that.

OUR UNIQUE GIFT

I have a wonderful dog, Jack. As I write this, he happily sits at my feet. I am pretty sure that Jack does not think much about the future. He does not live in a world of, "Maybe one day I'll get a bigger house and a better owner and more food and get to go on more walks." Nope. When I come through the door, Jack jumps on his haunches, puts his paws on my shoulders, and howls because he is so happy to see me. He greets me this way every time, and I'm grateful for it. It's nice to have Jack, who lives in the present. Human beings, though, almost have a superpower with their ability to visualize and see a different reality.

Looking to the future is a discernible capability of humans. It's an incredible gift, a superpower, even, if we let it be. What we do with that superpower is up to us.

That power comes from the brain's prefrontal cortex, which is highly analytical but is also able to create and imagine things that have never been imagined before. The more vivid the story, the more effective it is in creating that future. Think about good stories. You have to have a protagonist. You have to have barriers and obstacles that need to be overcome in order to get to the promised land, to take the hero's journey that Joseph Campbell spoke about in his book, *The Hero with A Thousand Faces*. Good stories evoke emotion, but they also engage our ability to envision and imagine the story. They must, to get us out of what we're currently doing.

Promoting hope is our way of writing our own compelling story, but those stories mean nothing without emotion. One of my clients recently received some negative feedback and as we discussed it, he showed little emotion. I was concerned because I know that hiding emotions can be internally destructive for us because eventually, those hidden emotions will find outlets to be expressed and often it is not very pretty. So, I tried to evoke with the client my own passion and emotion in an attempt to help him open up. I tried, really, to make him angry. Finally, he told me that his family runs a mortuary, and they were taught not to ever show any negative emotion. One of the strengths that this leader demonstrates is tremendous calm and kindness, but for him to use the constructive feedback he received for positive change, he may have to get upset with himself and passionately engaged in order to do something differently. We forget how wired we are as humans toward certainty and predictability and that to create change in our lives, we sometimes need to get mad with ourselves to have the courage to take another path. Additionally, when we have a vivid, compelling destination for ourselves, it can provide even more fuel for us to be willing to take the journey.

This manifests itself in many ways. I've been keenly interested in understanding why people stay in abusive relationships. Behaviorism tells us that when we touch a hot stove and get burned, we quickly learn not to touch hot stoves again. Yet, when you look at many battered spouses, often you find that what keeps them stuck is an inability to see themselves in a stable and happier future state, and they have immense self-doubt that they can make it on their own. This fear and self-doubt provides even greater motivation to stay in the abusive relationship where they would rather take their chances with being abused than deal with their deep fear of an uncertain future.

This habit, this unique power of promoting hope, can play a key role in helping counter that, but only if we are intentional about practicing and using it. Please don't misunderstand me. I am not saying that all a battered spouse has to do is to conjure up hope to escape their difficult situation. Thankfully, there are many organizations across America devoted to providing shelter and resources to battered spouses. And helping them develop a compelling, vivid, and exciting vision for their future selves is an important ingredient to leading a new life away from their abuser.

As we grow older, hopefully we grow wiser. That's my vision. But too often, we get more stuck in our ways. "You can't teach an old dog a new trick," right? Baloney. I want to be someone about whom my grandkids say to their parents: "You're not going to believe what the old guy is up to today!"

A professor at the University of Michigan, Robert Quinn, started the Center for Positive Organizations, where he employs, among other things, an exercise called the Reflected Best Self Exercise. The Reflected Best Self (RBS) Exercise has you reach out to those who know you in all contexts of your life and asks for stories and examples to help you understand and articulate who you are and how you contribute and impact others when you are at your best.

Most of us can recall our own extraordinary moments, those unique moments when we felt that our best self was brought to light, affirmed by others, and put into practice in the world. These memories are seared into our minds as moments in which we have felt truly alive and completely true to our deepest selves. The RBS Exercise can provide a portrait of who we are and what we do when we are at our personal best and is a tremendous resource we can draw upon to strengthen confidence and courage, face challenges, and step up to new responsibilities, as well as see possibilities for our future.

By knowing our strengths, we, in turn, can imagine a future self where those strengths are fully leveraged for great success, and because those strengths were affirmed in you already by those who engaged in the exercise, there is much greater probability for your future self to be realized because it is based upon what you already have and are committed to most fully developing and utilizing.

The RBS Exercise is beautiful because it's very affirming. It provides a blueprint for how you can bring your very best self into the future. Then, there's no excuse to not be your very best because you've done it before.

HOPE AND SUCCESS

Hope isn't just about having a clear vision of the future. It's about following through.

Remember Napoleon Hill? He's the guy who spent years observing successful people and unsuccessful people and discovering the most critical ingredients to success. As we discussed earlier, Hill showed us that there are three essential ingredients of success and all are related to hope.

The first ingredient was clarity of purpose. They had to have that confident, positive vision for the future. The second was discipline and the will to focus attention on that clarity of purpose, and the third quality was sustainability and persistence to keep focusing that attention toward the clarity of purpose, no matter what. The most successful were masters at envisioning a compelling and vivid future state and having the courage and tenacity to harness that hope and follow through to bring it to completion.

HOPE AND VISUALIZATION

Let's revisit Linda, the doctor who felt "stuck" and made "move" her theme for the year. She had gone through a transformative education experience, earning a master's in healthcare management. Through that, she saw what her future could look like. It also highlighted how dysfunctional her current work environment was, and she got very disappointed.

I asked her, "What could a great work environment look like? Let's try to make pieces of that as compelling as possible." I asked her to describe the best boss she could possibly have. I asked her to tell me about her colleagues and the type of work she would be doing in an ideal world, the changes she would get to be part of. I asked her to envision how she would be taking better care of herself and some of the hobbies and non-work pursuits that would bring her more joy and happiness.

My job was to keep her anchored around what was realistic but to also dream big. Once she dreamed big and we wrote it down, the vision became a beacon of light. Once she had the theme of movement, it was all enough to push her to let go of where she was and move enthusiastically toward what could be.

She was able to specifically envision how she would be valued and respected at work and gain a reputation as a person of influence. She ran into the CEO of the new hospital she's at recently and the first thing he said was, "I've already heard so many wonderful things about you."

Another client, David, is a hospital CEO. I challenged David to visualize five years down the road the impact he wanted to have on those he served as CEO. He also got vividly clear about the quality of his relationships with his family and the people he loved. He started speaking publicly and cultivating his purpose and gratitude. He is one of the most genuinely kind and thoughtful people I've ever worked with. His sense of purpose, his big why, was rooted in humble service to others and the mission of the organization he was entrusted to lead.

Because he had so much talent and his values ran so deep, I knew David would be able to influence others in ways he couldn't even imagine. I asked him to visualize where he needed to invest in his growth and development so that he could be as influential as possible. Five years from now, I asked him, what does life look like for you and how are you showing up as a leader, as a father, as a husband? And then how do we get there? What do you need to start doing today to bring those visions to fruition?

I came to see the power of the habit of promoting hope through my own practice of it over the last fifteen years. I have been very deliberate at keeping five-year descriptions of my life that will keep me excited, energized, and engaged. Here is what I wrote over the holidays last year to describe my life at sixty-three in the year 2022.

- I have healthy, supportive, vibrant, trusting, and respectful relationships with Claudia, Erik, Emily, Katie, Molly, Jerome, Brad, Felicity, our grandchildren, mother-in-law, siblings and their families, colleagues, friends, and clients that I am actively involved with. I bring to all of my relationships a non-anxious presence, humility, compassion, kindness, generosity, and integrity.

- I give generously to others and am committed to the wild success of my wife, children, family, friends, business colleagues, and clients.
- I am focused, purposeful, and persistent in accomplishing those tasks, objectives, and goals that I have committed to. I continually renew my mind through reading, reflecting, writing, and engaging others in meaningful dialogue and learning.
- I continue to write and get published while being a sought-after speaker on topics of leadership, resiliency and change, joy and well-being.
- I am physically healthy, strong, at my ideal weight of 194 pounds, and have significant energy and vitality to sustain my active lifestyle and to share my talents and gifts with others.
- Claudia and I have rich social lives; we continue to take incredible vacations throughout the world. We also spend at least a third of the year in our home on the coast of North Carolina.
- I am living a life that is fulfilled by service and support to others by helping them grow, learn, and lead more effectively, and I am a catalyst for building responsible, effective, and compassionate leadership in the world.
- I am grateful to God for the gift of life and the opportunity to serve and support others. I strive to live my values all the time. I am successful when I am living authentically aligned and with integrity.

- I live in an attitude of great gratitude for the incredible life I have been given by God.
- I am intentional in choosing a purpose bigger than my own self-interests by: 1) Being a catalyst for building compassionate, responsible, and effective leadership in the world by daily investing in the lives of those I coach, educate, facilitate, and consult with. 2) Being a healing, joyful, and healthy presence to the organizations and people I serve. 3) Building and managing a company of like-hearted and like-minded individuals who are aligned with my purpose of investing in the lives of others to be more effective, responsible, and compassionate leaders.

I know that as long as I keep reviewing and reminding myself of this exciting and compelling future state, even my subconscious will be working on my side to bring my dream to reality.

My client David took the exercise of imagining his life five years out just as seriously, and it is exciting seeing how his life continues to unfold. We were together recently, and it was amazing to see how the future state he described and his desires are coming to fruition, piece by piece. In five years, David wants to have the opportunity to be a prominent speaker on issues of servant and compassionate leadership. He also openly admits that he is terrified of speaking. Yet, because David's vision is so compelling and he reflects on it often, he's finding more and more opportunities to speak. I tell others who know David that we will all be saying, "We knew David when..." and they smile and nod in strong agreement.

HOPE IN THE FACE OF STRUGGLES

I know that years ago I had this great hope that life would get easier and my struggles would come to an end. Thankfully, I have come to see that while I prefer not having any struggles, they are a necessary part of life and in all probability, when you no longer have struggles, you are close to pushing up daisies. Every struggle that comes into our life is an opportunity to learn something important. Struggles are like sandpaper, as they present the opportunity to polish our rough edges and truly move toward our better selves.

I asked a client recently, "On a scale of one to ten, how would you assess your joy and happiness today?" He thoughtfully pondered my inquiry and responded, "Regrettably, I feel like I am at a six and as you know that's not usually where I am at." In the past when I have asked him that question, he would respond enthusiastically, "easily an eleven."

He said he was in a hard place, that he was struggling. And my response was: "I am sorry that you are in a difficult place. What do you think your current struggles may be offering you in terms of your growth and learning? How can you use these struggles to help you be an even better you?" I was asking him to potentially reframe the impact of the current struggles in his life, to see that his struggles were offering something beyond just making life hard. We know that what makes diamonds is immense pressure. Many of us have heard the story of the little boy who watches the worm struggle to leave its cocoon, and decides to cut open the chrysalis to free the worm from its struggle. Unfortunately, the worm, now an undeveloped butterfly, falls to the ground, unable to fly. It needed to struggle to reach its true potential.

So, I asked my struggling client to consider viewing his challenging times as a wonderful, wise teacher, equipping him and helping him truly evolve into his very best self. Promoting hope certainly begins with a powerful and compelling purpose and destination, but sometimes the path to get there will present us with all sorts of wonderful and unexpected twists and turns. While we should stay true and fixed to our destination, the twists, turns, and struggles may be the very things that allow our journey to be fully realized.

REVISITING THE POWER OF STORY

Eighteen years ago, I attended a self-development

program called *The Freedom Course* (This was the self-improvement course I mentioned earlier in the book's introduction). I took away two important tools that have been transformative in my life. The first tool was being able to see how much of what happens in life is made up in our heads and in the stories we tell. We are always telling ourselves stories. This is how we make sense of a very complicated, complex world. If someone cuts me off in traffic, the story I instantly tell is that they're a jerk, right? The reality is that most stories are nothing more than interpretations. The guy who cut me off might be racing to the hospital because his loved one just had a heart attack. He could be leaving a place where he just got fired after fifteen years. We often don't know anyone else's story.

I have found extraordinary freedom from seeing myself tell a story and then telling a better story that comes with a lot less emotion and drama. Often, the things other people "do to you" have nothing to do with you at all. We often tell the wrong stories. I also love telling many of my clients that they should read the book, *What You Think of Me is None of My Business* by Terry Cole-Whittaker, as a funny way to remind them that sometimes we can take what others say or think of us far too seriously.

As I have shared before, because of my early childhood psychological wounds, I've been carrying a big story around with me called "Greg, the Unlovable, Worthless Failure." And gratefully, I have come to see that indeed it was a big fat story with virtually no shred of evidence or fact supporting it. A much more empowered story is that I was deeply loved by my parents and grew up in a very supportive environment in some of the most wonderful places in the world. And from an early age, I got good grades, excelled in sports, won awards for my musical talents, and frequently was the lead in plays and often picked by my classmates and superiors for roles of leadership. Indeed, I was also quite mischievous and rebellious and caused a lot of problems with my parents when I was young that I have come to believe came out of the terrible and false story I told myself.

When I work with others in supporting their efforts to change their self-care strategy (such as eat less; move, sleep, and meditate more; and add more joy), I ask them to envision their life ten or fifteen years from now in two stories. The first story is if they do nothing to take better care of themselves. The second story is one which reflects their significant changes in self-care. I ask them to be as clear and compelling as they can about both stories. Hopefully, the first story should create significant dissatisfaction. The second story, in turn, should give them a deep desire for something much better in their lives and helps them develop the hope and optimism to keep moving and motivated toward a wonderful future.

The picture of the two Nigerian girls I frequently look at helps me better appreciate what I have, and it also helps me reframe whatever story I'm telling myself about something that's challenging, or I am frustrated by. Once I remind myself of what the two girls endured, I conclude that my issue or problem is so insignificant in comparison. And just that shift helps remind me of all the good that has come into my life and because of that good, I have a great responsibility to do and be my best.

That makes it a lot easier to be hopeful.

GET HOPEFUL, AND GET BUSY

There's a quote I love from *Alice's Adventures in Wonderland*. Alice is talking to the Cheshire Cat, and they have the following exchange:

> *"Would you tell me, please, which way I ought to go from here?"*

> *"That depends a good deal on where you want to get to,"* said the Cat.

> *"I don't much care where..."* said Alice.

> *"Then it doesn't matter which way you go,"* said the Cat.

A sense of urgency helps create hope for the future. Urgency is about knowing what's important and directing energy toward that. If everything is important, nothing is. Live your life with intention.

The author Anne Lamott tells a beautiful story in her book, *Bird by Bird, Some Instructions on Writing and Life*, of a dear friend of hers who had terminal cancer. She decides to take her friend, who is in a wheelchair, shopping at an upscale department store. Lamott comes out of a dressing room and asks her friend how she looks in a new dress. Paraphrasing, her friend basically tells her, "Oh Annie, given the time I have left, we have so many more important things to talk about."

That story still resonates with me. Most of the things we get bent out of shape over steal energy we should be giving to the things that are truly important. We must be conscious and intentional about what matters most.

I spoke at the kickoff for a leadership program and shared my vision statement with the twenty-two new leaders who were there. I told them how I want to be compassionate and kind to everyone I meet. I told them how I want to be wildly generous to my family, my friends, and my clients. I shared that I developed these aspirations based upon envisioning my final days on earth and wanting to end my life on the highest notes possible. I've thought about what qualities I want people to mention about me after I am gone—kind, compassionate, generous, thoughtful, and purposeful. I also was quite honest about how these qualities did not come naturally to me and so I would have to be intentional and disciplined to achieve my aspirations and be vulnerable in asking people I value and respect for their feedback on my progress.

You have to decide what you want most from your one life. Decide well, and once you have decided, create the most compelling picture of your decision as possible. Make it so vivid and real that it excites and inspires you. Review and affirm it as often as possible. Create accountability partners who can help you realize your dreams and will be honest with you when you get off track.

Change is hard for human beings, even faced with monumental consequences. Creating a habit of promoting hope is so important because it provides a daily opportunity to reflect on the story you want to bring about in your life. The fifth habit is an opportunity each and every day to reflect on, "How do I live my life so that when I get to the end of the road, I have as few regrets as possible?"

REFLECTION AND ACTION

Before you move on to the next chapter, please consider reflecting on and writing down your responses to the following questions related to "Promoting Hope":

Your Best Possible Self: Reflect and write down what you expect your life to be a few years from now. (Think five or ten years from now.) Imagine that everything has gone as well as it possibly could. You have worked hard and succeeded at accomplishing many of your most important goals. *You are incredibly healthy, happy, and joyful. See it. Feel it. Think it. Dream it. Act toward it.*

....

....

....

Your Best Possible Day: Imagine what a great day looks like for you tomorrow. Describe it as vividly as possible, perhaps in half-hour chunks of time. See yourself happy, joyful, enthusiastic, positive, and resilient.

....

....

Chapter 10

BEING MINDFUL

Bill is the CEO of a growing defense contractor, and he asked me to help him take the company to the next level. He was already an exceptional leader with a good mind and a big heart. But his pace felt relentless. He was struggling with managing everything in his business while also struggling with helping one of his adult children, who continued to make bad choices and challenge Bill and his wife at seemingly every turn.

When I started working with him, we spent most of our time focusing on how to grow his company, but I could sense that he was feeling stuck regarding his own sense of well-being. He had enjoyed a successful career in the military but was medically discharged due to long-standing health challenges. It bothered him deeply that he was unable to complete his military service. He knew he needed to take better care of himself and that he needed to better develop a more thoughtful response to his challenging son, to include being calmer and less triggered by his son's actions.

We talked about ways he could better take care of himself. He had been a college swimmer and he had stayed pretty active. But the issues that had caused him to be medically discharged were making it more challenging for him to stay as active as he once was.

We talked about mindfulness and how important it was to spend time each morning in some level of stillness and quiet. He was reading the bestseller, *10% Happier: How I Tamed the Voice in My Head, Reduced Stress Without Losing My Edge, and Found Self-Help That Actually Works: A True Story* by Dan Harris and listening to Harris's podcasts on meditation. (By the way, could Dan come up with a longer title?) He decided he needed help in developing and maintaining a meditation practice and habit, and so we discussed the meditation app, Headspace, that had helped me get started in practicing meditation several months previously to our starting working together. He started getting up earlier and besides meditation, using the early uninterrupted hours of stillness to reflect more on his life.

I worked with Bill for two years and continued to be impressed with how his spending, on average, thirty minutes a day meditating and in quiet reflection brought him such peace and clarity in how to lead his business and respond in a more thoughtful, loving, and compassionate way to some of his family challenges.

Meditation and reflection for Bill became an important part of how to make each day as impactful and meaningful as possible. He told me, "Meditating helps bring calm to a sea of chaos."

For Bill, meditation and reflection is what worked to get him centered, clear, and focused on what was most important. Bill was learning to be more mindful and through that mindfulness, it helped him create even more clarity for himself and those he led and served in his business and family.

WHAT IS MINDFULNESS?

Mindfulness is often confused with meditation. Meditation is only one path to being mindful. There are many other paths, depending on the person. The aim is to be very intentional about making sure our minds and our lives are not filled with overwhelming pressure and stress and that our minds are clear and focused on what really matters most in our lives. In addition to sitting nonstop throughout the day looking at a computer screen, the second highest thief of people's lives is chronic stress and anxiety.

Being mindful is the cultivation of a sound and stable mind that's not constantly living in the frenetic pace of the rat race or in a place of pessimism, anxiety, and constant fear. When you're mindful, your mind is serving you, rather than you serving the mind. Anything that allows the mind to be focused—and not in a place of fear, tension, or anxiety—is a strategy for improved mindfulness.

One of the ways you can access mindfulness is having a hobby that allows you to do nothing but serve the hobby. One of my clients, for example, told me she uses a riding lawn mower to cut the grass on her two acres. For her, the noise and the movement of the riding mower creates a happy place, a sense of inner peace. She's in the moment. When she is mowing the grass, she is not thinking of anything else but taking in the sound of the mower, the smells of the cut grass, and whatever weather is showing up while she mows. That's mindfulness.

One of my clients has a small, tree-covered courtyard at work right outside his office. He goes there and just sits, enjoying the space, taking in the foliage and shade of the trees, to recharge his batteries and find stillness in the midst of busy, unrelenting days and work obligations. We will often have our coaching sessions out there; it's just a quiet, peaceful refuge. When he's out there, he finds peace and he grounds himself.

I have another client who loves to knit. When she knits, she enjoys the repetitive actions of her hands as she knits and purls her stitches in creating new pieces. She calls it "her therapy." Any strategy that helps you reestablish some quiet and calm as an antidote to the frenetic and crazy intensity of our work is an opportunity to be mindful.

Years ago, I bought a DVD from National Geographic called *Celebrate What's Right with the World*. Dewitt Jones, the creator of the DVD, is a famous photographer for *National Geographic* and *Outdoor Photographer*. The essence of the DVD was that sometimes in the hustle and bustle of our days we don't pay attention to the extraordinary beauty around us. One story from that DVD that has stuck with me for years is about a woman who had been named a Dame by Queen Elizabeth because of her great knitting skills. She lived in a tiny fishing village in Scotland. Dewitt thought it would be a good photo shoot, so he found the woman. While having tea in her cottage, he asked her, "When you're knitting these beautiful things, what are you thinking about?"

She said, "Aye, laddie. When I knit...I knit." I love to tell that story and it always gets a laugh from whomever I share it with because it is so simple and true. Her greatness as a knitter is because indeed that's what she is able to focus all of her attention on.

In other words, she's in the moment. She's present. There's nothing but herself and the knitting. That's mindfulness.

THE SCIENCE OF MINDFULNESS

As we learn more about the human mind and body, we are discovering the negative effects of cortisol, a hormone created through stress, on our longevity. If you study the people who live the longest and have the highest quality of life from the blue zones—Okinawa, Costa Rica, Icaria, Loma Linda, and Sardinia—you'll see that they have found wonderful ways to downshift through, and especially at the end of, their days. Their lives are not filled with things that have to get done before sunup to well after sundown. Anything that allows you to slow down is a strategy for mindfulness. Being still is an antidote. In all the world's religions, one of the most important pathways is being still. In that silence, we often get reconnected with the Divine, however we may define it.

In the beginning of the book, I spoke of Professor Richard Davidson, who is currently the director of the Laboratory for Affective Neuroscience, director of the Waisman Laboratory for Brain Imaging and Behavior, and the chairperson of the Center for Investigating Healthy Minds, all at the University of Wisconsin. He is best known for his groundbreaking work studying emotion and the brain. He has taken trips to Tibet and Northern India and is keenly interested in the deep meditative states of the Tibetan monks. He decided to explore that further, using sound techniques to capture their brainwaves. He asked a group of Monks to come to the University of Wisconsin, so he could study their brainwaves while they were in their deep meditative states. He was able to show that their brain neurons actually grew—something that had never been measured or recorded before. For many years, the belief was that our neural networks fully formed around the age of six or seven. This discovery was a big deal. He was able to demonstrate that when we cultivate our mind, we find greater peace and stability and we create an even healthier mind that expands in its capacity. Happiness, like any skill, requires practice and time, but because we now know that the brain is built to change in response to mental training, it is possible to train a mind to be happy and joyful.

I often tell healthcare leaders that the biggest demographic they need to be concerned about is the growing number of eighty-five- to ninety-five-year-olds. We are living longer, which is a wonderful thing, but unless we take better care of our minds and our bodies, we will see a deluge of dementia, Alzheimer's, and Parkinson's, the so-called mind diseases.

The newest research says you don't need four hours of meditation a day, like the Dalai Lama. Ten minutes will do. Like Bob, I used to use the Headspace app, and later switched to another app called Calm. Each of the apps has their strengths. For me, it was a preference of the meditation teacher's voice, as I found the voice on Calm to be much more soothing. And every day, it gives me a short meditation session focused on important areas such as reducing anxiety, managing stress, being grateful, and seeking calm. I find that even ten minutes of meditation can help me slow down, be calmer, and feel in greater control of my thinking and focus.

A recent study from the University of California in Berkeley showed that by creating a daily rhythm of meditation—just ten minutes a day—in just six weeks the restorative impact meditation had on people's mental, psychological, and emotional well-being was significant. Because of the wide acceptance of this kind of research, many companies in Silicon Valley, to include Google and Apple, provide onsite classes on meditation and mindfulness to their employees. They are seeing the enormous benefit to employee wellness and engagement.

MINDFULNESS IN THE MODERN WORLD

It has gotten harder to be mindful in the modern world with social media, the barrage of negative news, and other distractions in our increasingly fast-paced world. The political news cycle feels out of control, as throughout the day, some news channel will pronounce, "Breaking news" and offer us another "they said, no they didn't" saga of political discourse. We don't want to, but it is very easy to get sucked up by this media cycle where we're bombarded by emails, texts, tweets, Instagram, and Snapchats. It is even easier when our minds and bodies are exhausted, overwhelmed, and stressed out.

I was going up an escalator recently and noticed the people going down. Every single person was looking at a phone. I was in the airport train and saw the same phenomena. And even at a restaurant a few days ago, I noticed couples not talking to each other but peering into their phones, instead of looking at each other and having some meaningful dialogue and I thought, how sad that we as a society are seeing so much more value in reading something in our "smart" phones than being connected to another human being's presence.

There is a mindset that everything has to be faster. Our modern society can be intense. Americans get the least amount of vacation from their jobs each year of any developed country in the world, and many of us don't even use the vacation we're given. The second annual installment of Project: Time Off's "State of the American Vacation" study published in 2017, showed that American workers left behind 662 million unused vacation days in 2016, 4 million more days than in 2015. In the study, it also reported that more than half of American workers (54 percent) didn't use all of their vacation days, slightly less than the previous year (55 percent). When many of us do go on vacation, we are still working because we can be reached almost anywhere at any time.

Claudia and I love taking vacations that include riding bikes because when I'm riding eighty-nine miles from Bryce National Park to Zion in Utah in some of the most beautiful scenery in the world, I'm not checking my phone or working. And when I am riding in such beautiful places, where my experience would be described as "stunning, breathtaking, or exhilarating," I have to believe that these positive emotions are good for the mind, heart, and spirit. When I am on my bike, it's just me and the outdoors. The external world finds a larger presence within me when I'm seeing it from my bike. I lose the apparent need (worsened by social media and the constant barrage of news) to feel connected to the world through technology and instead feel connected to the world through seeing it, feeling it, and experiencing it.

If all you're doing is looking at the incessant news cycle and being bombarded by emails—if you're spending too much time connected to these external things—it can be a world where you feel highly anxious and fearful. Too often, that's our natural state. Being mindful is an antidote to this predisposition toward anxiety, fear, and tension.

Mindfulness alleviates that. Ninety percent of our thoughts are the same as yesterday. Mindfulness allows more space, so better thoughts can come through. We spend a lot of time thinking about the past. If you're not thinking about the past, you're probably worried about the future. Most of us aren't focused on the present. Eckhardt Tolle describes this in his bestseller, *The Power of Now*, published in 1997. The book was Buddhism repackaged. As the title indicates, Tolle makes a powerful case that since all we really have is this moment, our freedom and power comes from our ability to access the present, since we cannot undo or bring back the past and the future has not yet occurred.

Presence is so powerful and wonderful. When you're fully present with another person, we feel it.

CULTIVATING MINDFULNESS

To cultivate mindfulness, first you need to know it is integral to your well-being. As I have written previously, the human condition is to be often in a place of fear, stress, and anxiousness, and we have to understand the consequences of living constantly in that place. It leads to shorter lives and lives of less quality. It's not just awareness but changing our natural tendency to be in a state of peace and stillness. Research shows our sleep is affected by stress as well. Even while our bodies are trying to sleep, our minds are still working. We're worried about the things that need to happen the next day and the potential threats. When we don't cultivate mindfulness, it leads to stress and anxiety during the day but also sleeplessness at night.

The importance of sleep cannot be understated.

I was with a new client recently, Ted, and it was a challenging interaction because Ted and his spouse had not cultivated many habits besides working and raising children. Now that their kids are grown and moving on with their own lives, they are also struggling with their own identities. They don't have many hobbies, nor do they enjoy travel.

Ted opened up to me, "I'm not sure my life will have a good ending." That statement gave me great concern for his well-being and he could sense that, so he quickly shot back, "I don't mean that I will do anything drastic; I just am not sure I can change this trajectory I have been on." The quality of his relationships with others (besides his children) was not great, including with his wife. He was not doing much to take care of his health, and besides being a successful leader in his organization, he cultivated very little else in his life.

I try not to offer advice or provide judgment to my clients and instead ask the right questions that will allow for their own discernment and insights on how they can create more productive, happier, and joyful lives. At this time, I did not follow this path. Instead, I shared, "No, that's not right, you have an enormous ability to make positive change in your life. You have been too successful in your professional life not to have similar success in your personal life. It is a matter of choice. Now, I know it will be hard and require determined work to see that choice fulfilled, but you have everything at your disposal to do that work." I think he was a bit surprised by my passion and directness, but he did listen, and he even acknowledged that I was right. I was very grateful for that because when you give people hard-hitting messages, they are often not received well.

But Ted reminds me that we don't have to keep making the same choices. We can change our lives, starting today, starting now. It takes a while for people to forgive us, but if they can see consistency of changed behavior and our renewed commitment to our relationship with them, anything is possible.

The first step to cultivating mindfulness is to acknowledge that you can train and strengthen the mind. This is hard because humans crave certainty and comfort. The path of least resistance for most humans is to keep doing what we've always been doing. George Bernard Shaw said youth is wasted on the young. As we age, if we do increase in wisdom, our bodies are decaying. So, the older we get, the harder it is to change whatever trajectory we're on.

When you are ready to begin, start small. Headspace starts people at three-minute meditations and builds them up to longer sessions. Anyone can do it for three minutes. From there, build slowly and regularly.

As I have shared before, I often recommend to clients to use a program like Headspace or Calm to get their meditation practice jumpstarted. Like the Gratitude365 app, these apps provide summaries of how long you've been doing it. It's a reminder of the work you've put in. It's worked for me and so many others. As I did my meditation with Calm this morning, I enjoyed seeing a four-day streak on the app's calendar. Those visual cues help us create better habits.

As I indicated before, mindfulness does not equate to meditation and if meditation is not your thing, there are hundreds of other strategies you can use to cultivate your mind's ability to slow down, be still, find quiet, and seek peace. For example, one way that I cultivate mindfulness is by playing piano and singing. It's not being still, but when I am playing and singing, my mind is not worried about what I have to get done. It's just thinking about the joy I get from the experience, and for those moments, for me, the world is a happy place.

If you're not sure, there are activities you can join. My daughter, Emily, teaches yoga and she weaves mindfulness into her classes, but for many activities—tennis, martial arts, bowling, fishing, you name it, mindfulness is an inherent part of it. Find the happy place where you find a little more of yourself.

Of the seven habits, being mindful equips us with greater capacity to manage our emotions, to make better choices, to be intentional about having as remarkable and meaningful a life as possible. And it is indeed about a choice for me to be at my very best.

IN THE CHAPTER: "BEING MINDFUL"

Before you move on to the next chapter, please consider reflecting on and writing down your responses to the following questions related to "Being Mindful":

Being mindful is simply the act of paying more attention to the present moment, be it your thoughts, your feelings, or your experience of what's happening around you. We find it by taking small pockets of time each day to de-stress and create some emotional and mental distance from all of the swirling demands on our time, energy, and attention.

As you reflect on the following activities and ones not listed that might bring about mindfulness, what opportunities do you have throughout your day to be more mindful even in the midst of the swirl and demands of busy, full days?

Prayer

Reading for Fun

Meditation

Knitting

Deep breathing

Coloring, drawing, or even doodling

Reflecting on beauty

Remembering a wonderful memory of a place, person, and/or time

Envisioning a future place of calm, serenity, and peace

Others?

What would it look like in your daily life to create small pockets of protected time to be more mindful? What will it take to become a daily habit?

$$=====\ Chapter\ 11\ =====$$

GET MOVING

Calvin is a busy executive with a young family. Like many of my clients, he works long days, has important responsibilities, and is very committed to doing a great job for those he serves and leads. He tries to get a head start on the day by arriving to work early, and because he has a great sense of responsibility to his organization, he often stays late. He works extremely hard, but physically he wasn't taking very good care of himself, and his body, mind, and overall well-being were paying for it. Despite all the long hours he put in, very few of them were dedicated to exercising or, as I prefer to call it, movement.

Calvin is a military veteran, so he's no stranger to physical fitness. He was even on the varsity basketball team in college. But like so many of us, as the years ticked by, staying active while managing busy work and family lives got more and more challenging.

We all have our reasons for not being as active as we know we should be. There aren't enough hours in the day, we say. It's too hard to stick with it. We're tired. It's the kind of thing you do when you're younger. For Calvin, his mindset about exercise was that if he wasn't working out hard for an hour and breaking a heavy sweat, why bother?

Often, I draw a circle with my clients and I say, "Let's say within this circle represents all the things you need to do to care for yourself. Where would you put sleep?" Of course, everyone says sleep deserves a spot in the circle. Without sleep, you'd be a mess, right? Then, I ask them where to put eating; they all say eating gets a spot in the circle. What about movement, I ask? Too often, people put movement outside the circle. "Why?" I ask, "wouldn't the research tell us that living an active lifestyle that includes significant movement is essential for our well-being?" "Of course," they agree.

So I challenged Calvin to bring movement back into his life, first by starting small. So, he started doing push-ups and a few calisthenics to start his day. It took ten minutes, but it created momentum for him. Creating that momentum, that habit, even as small as it was, helped him to get started. From there, he continued to build, forming a fun support network with colleagues that helped him (and them) stay motivated and keep at it.

Research says movement is unbelievably important to the

longevity and quality of your life. From the Blue Zones, one of the "Power Nine" strategies for maintaining a long, active life is to seek opportunities every day to keep moving. Okinawans are famously long lived; the women there have the greatest life expectancy in the world at ninety. Per capita of population, there are more centenarians on Okinawa than anywhere else, five times more than in the rest of Japan, and that's a high bar. Rates of cancer, stroke, coronary heart disease, and depression are well below the average of other advanced economies, yet they don't go to gyms nor do they jog. Instead, you can see elderly Okinawans working in their vegetable gardens, practicing tai chi, and riding bikes. Additionally, most Okinawans' homes typically don't have conventional furniture; they prefer to sit and sleep on the floor. And because of that, most Japanese women are constantly having to use their leg and arm muscles throughout the day to get up and down in their homes while frequently going outside to tend to their gardens and socialize with their friends and family. We see similar patterns of behavior in Costa Rica, Icaria, and Sardinia where there are great communal norms of frequent movement to join gatherings of friends and family at numerous times of the day and early evening.

As I mentioned before, the five Blue Zones enjoy temperate climates allowing for year-round movement outdoors and so certainly that plays a part of it. American society does not do as well to make it easy for people to walk and gather outdoors. Several years ago, as I had two of my adult daughters move back to Atlanta, Claudia and I made a difficult decision to sell our house in the North Atlanta suburbs and move to downtown Atlanta, so we could live in close proximity to our daughters and their growing families. Where we live in Atlanta is a very nice enclave, Virginia Highlands, where we are within easy walking distance of many wonderful restaurants. And because there are sidewalks everywhere, there is a more accepted culture of people out and about walking and enjoying the outdoors. Where we used to live in Marietta is the land of the subdivisions and even when there were suitable sidewalks, very few used them. We were fortunate to live very close to a beautiful YMCA fitness center that my family frequently used. What is interesting to me, though, is that the center was probably no more than a quarter mile from my home and I can count the number of times my family or I walked to it on one hand, always deciding to drive for convenience. If that same YMCA fitness center was located near my new home, the decision to walk or drive would be completely the opposite where we would walk with joy to the center. The point of that story is we often don't realize how our behavior is being shaped by cultural and societal norms and expectations and to live a remarkable life, you must consciously and intentionally build habits that will promote well-being, joy, happiness, and resiliency.

WHY MOVEMENT MATTERS

I often give my clients a book called *Spark: The Revolutionary Science of Exercise and the Brain* by Dr. John Ratey, a well-known Harvard psychiatrist, who became famous in the 1990s for his work on Attention Deficit Disorder in adults. *Spark* goes into study after study of the importance of exercise on brain health. Most of us realize that exercise helps our bodies function better, but not all of us have made the same connection to brain health. Exercise is a huge prophylactic against brain diseases such as Alzheimer's and dementia.

When we exercise, we know it builds more muscle or more stamina. Many of us have the experience of how daily exercise, such as running a few miles or climbing stairs, becomes easier if we do it regularly.

When it comes to our brain, though, the connection is less understood. While we have all heard the phrase, "endorphins are released," this is what actually happens in our brains when we exercise. When you start exercising, your brain recognizes this as a moment of stress. As your heart rate increases, the brain thinks "fight or flight." To protect yourself from stress, your brain releases a protein called BDNF (Brain-Derived Neurotrophic Factor). BDNF has a protective function and also reparative impact on your memory neurons and acts as a reset switch. This is why we often feel much more at ease and things seem much clearer after exercising. At the same time, endorphins, another chemical to fight stress, are released in your brain. Your endorphins' main purpose is to minimize the discomfort of exercise, block the feeling of pain, and produce feelings of euphoria. Overall, there is a lot more going on inside our brains when we move and stay active than when we are just sitting down. Neuroscientists are continuing to discover that this movement is essential to health, vitality, and well-being.

One of the antidotes to a world filled with information overload, anxiety, and stress, is being able to have sufficient energy to find the "pause." We've talked about this with mindfulness, but it's also true of exercise. When we're exercising, it's much harder to focus on one's fears, anxieties, and challenges. Claudia says that I am overly obsessive with exercise and to be honest, I think I am addicted to the calm and euphoria I experience when I am finished. As I usually exercise first thing in the morning, I also feel that I have gotten something very important accomplished and it sets up the first victory of my day with positive expectations that more are to follow.

The more we cultivate self, physically and mentally, the more capacity we have to be aware of the space, and then the greater capacity to thoughtfully choose our response. In a world that's moving faster, having a fit body and mind is a way to counter the stress and fatigue of modern society.

A *Wall Street Journal* article echoes this idea. According to the story, at the University of Virginia, students were invited to exercise and engage in social activities. The more they did, the better they felt about themselves and of course created the virtuous cycle that I have discussed throughout the book. From *Spark*, Dr. Ratey opens the book with a story about a school district south of Chicago, Naperville, where officials brought back mandatory Physical Education for all of its high schools. It's not just any PE, though; it's PE that gets the heart rate up to include a requirement for students to run a mile for time once a week. Not only is the run timed, but all students wear heart monitors so that their heart rates can be tracked. Grades are not given on how fast you run but on how hard you push yourself and the progress you make each week. The positive outcomes cannot be understated. Not only are Naperville's science and math scores competitive with some of the highest rates in the world; there is less violence and student conflict; and students rate their happiness and engagement with life as higher!

Naperville is an upper middle-class community, but this initiative has been done in other less affluent school districts with similar results. Now, some schools are suggesting kids do some kind of exercise before taking their college preparation exams such as the SAT and ACT, as exercise has been shown to tremendously increase one's focus and thinking.

It is never too late to start a habit of regular movement. Researchers from the University of British Columbia did 150 studies on elderly adults on how physical activity affects the risk for dementia and Alzheimer's. Their research concluded that older people who exercise regularly have a significantly lower risk of developing progressive brain disorders.

MOVE MORE, LIVE LONGER

A *Time.com* report in June said researchers analyzed 6,000 adults based on their physical activity and biological markers of aging. They used DNA samples to measure the lengths of participants' telomeres. As we discussed earlier in the book, telomeres shrink with age, as we lose bits of them every time a cell divides and those with shorter telomeres die sooner and are much more likely to develop chronic diseases.

Taking into account risk factors such as smoking, alcohol, and obesity, researchers found within these 6,000 results, that people who moved strenuously for 30 minutes, 5 days a week, have longer telomeres and on average a 9-year biological age advantage over sedentary adults. Those who moved a little less strenuously had a two-year age advantage.

In America, we're all about convenience. We give people

scooters. We use electric can openers. We even have devices that will put our socks on. Taking away the need for movement and resistance lowers the quality and longevity of our life. We can and must do better.

Making movement a priority in our lives is not just about living longer; it's about living well. Now, we have scientific proof that says a life of non-movement will take years off our lives and in our waning days of life, we will not have the mind or body health to enjoy the lives we do have.

MAKING THE HABIT

There is yet to be a study that says movement is bad for you. And yet, of the seven habits, it's the hardest one to start. Why?

Probably because it's hard, it takes time, and we feel like we don't have the energy. What we fail to realize (or conveniently overlook) is that moving and exercising more actually gives us *more* energy. Movement doesn't drain your gas tank; it increases the size of your gas tank.

As a young military officer in 1981, I came into the Army as America was still engaged in the Cold War with Russia and China. I had the privilege of being assigned to the only American Army Airborne unit in Europe and if war started, it would probably be in Europe. My unit's role was to parachute into harm's way to slow down the advance of the enemy so that America's military could be marshaled as quickly as possible. We believed we would only be a speed bump to slowing down the Russians and Iron Block countries, yet we were deeply committed to that mission. One of the ways for us to be as effective as possible was to make sure we were physically fit. Every day, if we weren't deployed, we would start our day with hard, physical training. It was an amazing way to start the day. It did become addictive.

And it still is.

That's the great thing about movement. It's the hardest to start but can be one of the easiest to keep going. When you start to feel (and see) the results, there is more motivation to keep going.

I wrote before that I wear my workout clothes to bed. Those have been my "pajamas" ever since I was a cadet at West Point. The message is deeply engrained in my head that when I wake up in the morning, I'm going to work out.

I started my habit of morning movement when I was at West Point. As my first year was stressful and demanding, I found morning movement as a means to lessen that stress, as well as improve my resilience. I certainly didn't use those words to describe why I did what I did. For me, it was very simple. After exercising I felt better, happy, and ready to face whatever would come my way. Now at fifty-eight, I think it is even more important in keeping my body and mind sharp, healthy, and resilient. And so, I get up most days and either at home, or in a hotel gym, ride a stationary bike or do resistance and strength training. Chances are, I also put my exercise down in my Gratitude365 app as something I am very grateful for and invariably, exercising and being grateful for that exercise, helps me cultivate even more positive emotion.

Good habits like movement are hard to create but once created they can sustain us in the toughest of times and challenges. While I will go into great depth in the next chapter regarding the science and power of habits, I want to challenge you to make this habit of movement a key priority in your self-care intentions. If not for yourself, do it for the people who love you, count on you, and want you to live long and well. At some point, most of us want to retire or at least slow down in the latter part of our lives so that we can better enjoy and savor the sweetness of life. I hear story after story of those who have moved into their retirement years but, because they have not taken good care of their bodies and minds, are unable to fully enjoy the fruits of their labors. The great news is that research is actually showing us that even those in their late 70s and 80s can start a movement habit, and the habit is helping them live life with greater vitality.

REMEMBER THE SCIENCE

It's important to be knowledgeable about what the research says, understand its impact, and be intentional about putting movement inside the circle of our lives. But knowing and doing are two different things. We must make movement as important as eating and sleeping.

You have to remember that movement belongs in your circle.

Regrettably, scientific data is not enough to motivate people to move more. The only thing that motivates people is positive emotion. We need social support, celebration, and community to help us get started and develop the habit.

So how do we create a movement plan? This is where the heavy lifting comes in. (No pun intended!)

IDENTIFY THE BARRIERS

First, set an intention to make meaningful movement a part of your life. Diagnose what the current barriers are and then come up with a plan to overcome them. Of course, always the first barrier I hear from people is a lack of time. Yet, make the case to yourself that we all have the same amount of time given to us, but we can create more energy in our lives if we make thoughtful investments in our mental, emotional, spiritual, and physical parts of our lives. When we make something a key priority, it is remarkable how creative we can get in making sure that priority is focused on and achieved.

Another barrier I hear from clients is that they have no access to equipment or a nearby gym. The great news is that just like those in Costa Rica and Okinawa, you don't have to run and you don't need barbells to stay active and keep moving. Research tells us that brisk walking is incredibly beneficial. Outdoor gardening and yard work are wonderful activities for muscle resistance and movement.

Some people might need a trainer or a gym with classes with people counting on you to show up. So that when you're ready to hit the snooze button, you say, "No, Suzy and Bob are counting on me."

START SMALL

Set yourself up for success by starting small. Start in ways where you feel the success of completing whatever small workout you decide to do. Find a fitness app that will give you positive reinforcement for even making the effort, and then string several days together.

Find what's going to work for you. Start small. Create a habit.

If running seems like a good fit, for example, don't start with the goal of running a marathon. Maybe start with your block.

Charles Duhigg talks about a woman in his book, *The Power of Habit*, who did just that. Movement was part of her plan to quit smoking, and she accomplished this through tiny steps. Her first step was to run around the block. Just one block. Then, having done that, she wondered: what would it look like to make the block longer?

As she began to create a pattern of running, she was able to confront her cigarette smoking. The two couldn't coexist. She found such a positive benefit from running that it gave her the fortitude to find the discipline to start eliminating smoking while she continued to run. But she had to build that over time, starting with just one block. It didn't come overnight.

HAVE FUN

Pick movement that you will enjoy, and be creative. We're not all meant to run marathons. You don't necessarily have to join a gym. Find something where you feel comfortable. If you hate the treadmill, go for a walk outside. Ride a horse. One of my clients, Dawn, hadn't ridden a horse for years, and decided to incorporate riding a horse at least twice a week. She truly loves it. So she's back to riding several times a week. And when she rides, she is actually practicing four of the seven habits. She is of course practicing movement. And she is also being mindful while riding, as she is able to put aside whatever pressures from her work and just ride to ride. Because this activity gives her so much joy, she also is cultivating positive emotion. She is extremely grateful she has taken the time to bring something she really loves back into her life. I know I was grateful when I received a text from her with a picture of her riding. It said, "Here I am, in my happy place." So movement doesn't have to look like traditional exercise. Find what works for you, brings you joy, and can be sustained, so it becomes part of the fabric of your life.

FIND YOUR COMMUNITY

Building on his initial momentum of starting his day with ten minutes of push-ups and calisthenics, Calvin started a healthy competition with his colleagues to see who could log the most sit-ups and push-ups. He was proud of how he'd gone from zero exercise to something he was committed to expanding in his life, and seeing the positive effects it was having. He found research on the immense value of twenty- to thirty-minute High Intensity Interval Training workouts (HIIT), a cardiovascular exercise strategy that alternates short periods of intense anaerobic exercise with less intense recovery periods, and started incorporating a few HIIT workouts each week. He felt more energized and refreshed—and he found out that there was indeed a way to work it into his very busy and demanding days.

The woman who started Weight Watchers, Jean Nidetch, came up with the idea of social support after she got tired of starting and stopping diets. She thought social support could be a way to provide her encouragement and accountability. Her initial idea was that each week, participants would go to a public weigh-in where everyone could see their weight. If weight goals were achieved, your accountability community would celebrate your progress and success. If you did not achieve your goals, the community would provide you with positive affirmation, encouragement, and support. This helps with accountability. Nobody wants to show up at the weigh-in having stayed the same or gained weight. While publicly weighing in might sound frightening, it is done in an encouraging environment. People have friends giving them encouragement and praise at the weigh-ins. The praise is external motivation.

CrossFit is another example of encouragement and support. It shifts from an exercise class to a social group. Your closest friends become your gym buddies. I have several friends that have completely changed their lives through their deep commitment to their CrossFit community.

When you encounter others who have been transformed like this, you are struck by not only the changes in them physically, but emotionally as well to include being more enthusiastic in life and having the energy and vitality to pursue other challenging goals and opportunities. One feeds the other.

Like with the types of activity you choose, you can also be creative with your support system, too. Weight Watchers participants celebrate their success. CrossFit gives you buddies at the gym. For Calvin, his was in-office competition. Find what works for you, but find a community that can give you positive support and accountability.

If I don't have a trainer or a class and it's just me and I don't like exercise, it's easy to decide to skip my workout. But if I've got my friends at the gym texting me asking where I am, I don't want to let my friends down. It's a nice accountability system.

REWARD YOURSELF FOR HARD WORK

Keeping track of my movement keeps me motivated to exceed my personal bests. It builds confidence as well as health. I feel more accomplished and vibrant at fifty-eight years old than I ever have.

I keep a Fitbit on my wrist and am constantly tracking

my steps. My Fitbit gives me positive affirmation as I hit key thresholds. Fitbit allows others to track me and vice versa. Claudia gave me a wonderful present for our thirty-seventh wedding anniversary, a Peloton stationary bike (I think she wants me to live long and be healthy). The Peloton allows me to take actual spinning classes being conducted around the country, or also take scenic trips to places like Costa Rica, France, or Big Sur. My output is always being compared against my best ride as well as all those who are taking the class or have done the ride in the past. I find that to be very motivating as my Peloton gives me a congratulatory message every time I hit a certain achievement. The positive affirmation keeps these habits going. The more you do, the more benefit you derive, the more you want to do it, and the more it just becomes part of the fabric of your life.

Additionally, my two sisters, Theresa and Julie, also have Pelotons, and we follow each other. Just the other day, Theresa sent us a text with a picture of her holding a sign indicating she had just completed her 200th ride. We congratulated her and the next day, I made sure I rode and celebrated my 150th ride, sharing the progress with my sisters. So, my sisters have become a bit like my accountability group, and I am grateful for their encouragement and support.

A necessary part of any good habit is to have a reward.

People who have the best habits around movement expand their rewards. For example, Claudia and I are already planning a bike trip to Croatia in June with a company that specializes in organizing these things. These bike trips have tremendous amounts of celebration built into the week. When you end a long trip, you celebrate. Celebrating is just another word for a positive reward and affirmation experience.

YOU'RE NOT ALONE

Again, movement may be the toughest habit to start. But it can be done, and you, like many of my clients, will realize that it's not the burden you think it is. In fact, you'll feel better than ever.

A client, Stephanie, and I started working together approximately a year ago. At our first meeting, she talked about the stress and sense of overwhelm of having a hard job, as well as many demands from home. She indicated that she was often exhausted. In our first session, I asked what she could do to take better care of herself, and one of the areas she committed to was frequent exercise.

The next month when we met she shared quite excitedly that she had been working out most mornings over the month, and she found it to be enormously helpful in giving her more energy and more willpower to better manage her time and busy life. She shared, "I can't thank you enough for encouraging me to work out before I start the day. I am sleeping better. I am less sluggish during the day and I find that I have more energy to stay focused." She also shared that she's a better leader, a better mom, and a better wife. She overall feels much better about herself. Now, if she has a meeting at 7 a.m., she'll get up at 5 a.m. because she has seen the benefit of starting her day with movement. Not everyone can start their day at 5 a.m., but if you could just be in the presence of Stephanie and hear her reflect on all the benefits that have come into her life because she starts her day with a habit of movement, I am convinced you would say to yourself, "I want what she has!"

For years, my client, Duane, has struggled with consistently exercising. Recently, he's proud that he has finally, after many months of encouragement and support, joined the YMCA and hired a trainer. He finally thinks movement is a habit he can sustain. He pays the gym membership (that's an incentive for him to use the gym), he pays the trainer (further incentive for him to meet the trainer and do the workout at the gym), and as his wife recently lost a loved one in her family, he goes to the gym so that he has the energy to be supportive to his wife as she is going through the grieving process. He even asked a colleague in his company to be his accountability partner, and every week they talk and share their progress. Duane and I meet once a month, and we have agreed to discuss his habit of movement every time we are together. I have been deeply impressed by his commitment but also his recognition that it would probably take a community of support and accountability to sustain his commitment and make it a habit.

I was with Duane recently and I commented, "You look great. It looks like you are sustaining that movement habit. Congratulations!" He appreciated the affirmation and he nodded with a smile, "You know it hasn't been easy, but I know it is good for me and I am committed to staying at it." I responded, "I know you will."

Humans are meant for movement and to be in a community. Celebration is a way to be intentional about enjoying the ride and the journey with the people we care about.

Find ways to get and keep moving. Make sure your story is as wonderful as possible and make movement an integral part of that story.

REFLECTION AND ACTION

Before you move on to the next chapter, please consider reflecting on and writing down your responses to the following questions related to "Get Moving":

What are the opportunities in your life for movement throughout your day?

....

....

What will it take to make movement a core habit for you?

....

....

Who can provide you with social support so that your habit has an opportunity to really get started and sustained?

....

....

What accountability systems do you need to sustain a meaningful habit of movement?

....

....

$=$ *Chapter 12* $=$

CREATING HABITS

Why are good habits so hard to create?

Habits are formed from repetition. After we do something long enough, it becomes part of the fabric of our lives. Habits that are bad for us—like smoking, drinking, or overeating—often make us feel good, so we're reluctant to give them up. To quit smoking, we often need to find another habit that makes us feel just as good. We're seeking the positive benefit without the negative effects.

We have an obesity problem in our country, for example, because of our habit of eating too much sugar and consuming too many empty calories. Many of us get addicted to all the pleasure we get from food and we eat more of it than we should. The signal from our stomach to our brains that we're full travels slowly, so in addition to eating too much of the wrong thing, we eat far too much of everything. In the Blue Zones, another "Power Nine" is being careful of how much we consume. The author, Dan Buettner writes that a 2,500-year-old Okinawan Confucian mantra, *Hara Hachi Bu,* said before meals reminds them to stop eating when their stomachs are 80 percent full. The 20 percent gap between not being hungry and feeling full could be the difference between losing weight or gaining it. People in the Blue Zones eat their smallest meal in the late afternoon or early evening and then they don't eat any more the rest of the day. So, in the meantime, many of us keep eating. Replacing ice cream with asparagus is hard.

So, we have to be more creative with the good habits, especially at the start, because the healthy habits may not give us the immediate positive feeling we're used to. It's like the famous marshmallow experiment conducted more than forty years ago. The Stanford marshmallow experiment was a series of studies on delayed gratification in the late 1960s and early 1970s led by psychologist Walter Mischel, then a professor at Stanford University. In these studies, a child was offered a choice between one small reward provided immediately or two small rewards (i.e., a larger later reward) if they waited for a short period, approximately fifteen minutes, during which the tester left the room and then returned. The reward was sometimes a marshmallow, but often a cookie or a pretzel. In follow-up studies, the researchers found that children who were able to wait longer for the preferred rewards tended to have better life outcomes, as measured by SAT scores, educational attainment, and even body mass index (BMI).

Habit creation has a lot to do with grit, and grit is about delayed gratification. It's about staying true to long-term goals in the midst of distraction and adversity. Good habits have a longer return than bad habits.

I wear my gym clothes to bed because it's a habit, a good habit that supports me in working out first thing in the morning. I've been doing it now for forty years, and it's greatly helped me, when I'm frequently travelling, to maintain decent levels of personal fitness and well-being. But, I know that for many others, keeping a habit of exercise can be very challenging. From January to March when I'm travelling to client locations, I have to be intentional about getting to the hotel gyms well before 6 a.m. so I can use their fitness equipment. It's hard after 6 a.m. because the people who set New Year's resolutions to lose weight or exercise more are often there, too, competing for the equipment. After March, though, I know I can sleep in a bit, arriving even after 6 a.m., and still get a stationary bike or elliptical machine because usually those with their New Year's resolutions have stopped coming. Research studies have shown that only 7 percent of New Year's resolutions are actually sustained. For the other 93 percent, the habits they are trying to create, even with the best intentions, often don't stick.

And my sense, while it's only empirical, is that it seems to be getting worse. Over the last few years, I have not seen the increase in gym users from January through March. My guess is it's because more and more people are deciding New Year's resolutions aren't worth making. It may be that we're getting even worse in this country at cultivating good habits. If you look at obesity rates state by state, it is a bit depressing that despite all we know about the lethal health implications of obesity, we as a nation cannot seem to hold the tide against this disease. And while we have finally made great inroads against smoking in our country, it took tremendous resources to include great government and societal collaboration to make that happen. Regrettably, we seem to be losing the war against drugs, especially opioids.

As humans, we are wired for efficiency. The brain wants to store energy for the next threat. This is why creating new habits is challenging and keeping old habits is easy. It's why we sleep in when we should get up, why we store fat instead of burning it.

The prefrontal cortex is easily taxed and easily overwhelmed. We're constantly overtaxing our minds, and because of that, it's harder to engage our minds in new habits.

A CASE STUDY

My client, Duane, whom we met in the last chapter, was incredibly motivated and did a lot of hard work to help him be more healthy and happy. Right away, he embraced the habits of social bonds and mindfulness. He was even making a choice to pay for my services out of his own pocket because his organization did not provide financial support for executive coaching. Because he had tremendous "skin in the game" he was extremely motivated to make the most of our time together and to actually put to use meaningful insights we discussed in order to help him be as successful as possible.

Duane has always been driven to achieve. For him, having an executive coach has been helpful, as it makes him more accountable, challenges him to expand his perspective, and provides him with deeper insight on how to be more effective. He has shared that he lives with greater intention after our monthly coaching sessions and he has taken to heart the majority of insights and lessons that this book contains.

For example, Duane knew the importance in his life of developing deeper bonds of friendship with others, and he got very intentional about expanding his network and building deeper friendships. He examined and better clarified his sense of purpose, created a ritual each morning to specifically cultivate more positive emotions, started keeping a gratitude journal, had a very clear vision and hope for his future, and explored ways to find greater stillness and peace by being more mindful.

Where he struggled was incorporating movement into his very busy and demanding life.

I understood why. Since his early thirties, Duane had experienced major health challenges to include a brain tumor that almost took his life. Other health challenges continue to plague him, and making movement a habit is more challenging than it might be for someone with a different health history. Additionally, he has a busy family consisting of his wife and three very young children that also require time, attention, and focus.

The point is, movement is hard for many of us. Even for someone as motivated as Duane, there was a major hurdle blocking his way toward cultivating a particular habit. Some habits are going to be harder than others to cultivate, depending on what we bring to the table. But that doesn't mean we give up.

To develop habits, we have to find something meaningful and valuable to associate with the habit. In other words, we need the proper motivation. He needed to have a reward, even if getting it meant it was harder for him to incorporate movement than most.

To Duane, movement wasn't fun. But as we discussed briefly in the last chapter, he and his wife are doing it together now. He has a gym membership and is paying a trainer to keep him engaged and focused. Recently, he told me he'd lost nineteen pounds, and he looks great. He and his wife take advantage of the childcare at the gym for their three children under five. They share their goals of successive workouts, weight loss, and other goals. For Christmas, he gave his wife dancing lessons for both of them. And when we last met, he spoke happily about the dancing class they had the night before. What an incredible way to incorporate not just movement into your life but the habit of deepening our social bonds and cultivating more positive emotions. Duane and his wife are enjoying a much better relationship and he's healthier, has more vitality, and of course, is much happier.

THE POWER OF HABIT

About six years ago, I was inspired by reading Charles Duhigg's *The Power of Habit: Why We Do What We Do in Life and Business*. Duhigg provides a very useful framework for understanding how habits are formed and what we can do to change them. *Habits are ultimately choices that you continue doing repeatedly without actually thinking about them.* At one point, they started with clear intention and a decision, but they eventually became automatic. They're very powerful and sometimes destructive. You can probably think about things you do every day that you wish you did less of (binging on Netflix shows, habitually opening Facebook, snacking when you're not hungry). But if you can understand how habits are triggered, you can overcome them. In short, you must set up a routine that gives you fast, positive feedback and keep doing it until it becomes a fully-formed habit. Good habits allow us to act and behave with good choices even when we are in periods of high stress and personal turbulence. We all know the lethal effects on our lives of bad habits.

Duhigg walks very carefully through the anatomy of a habit. A habit has three steps:

1. A cue, a trigger that tells your brain which habit to use and puts it into automatic mode.
2. A routine, which acts out the habit. This can be physical, mental, or emotional.
3. A reward, which is the result of the routine and reinforces the habit.

Experiments with rats in mazes show this in its most simplistic form. Put a rat in a maze, with a piece of cheese as its reward at the end of it. When you release the rat in the maze, you play a click sound. The first time, the rat explores randomly and eventually finds the cheese. You repeat this multiple times, with the same click at the same time, and the cheese in the same place and over time, the rat gets conditioned (or builds a habit) to follow the correct route to the reward, every time. The click is the cue that activates the routine, or the specific route through the maze that gets to the cheese reward.

You can even condition the rat to activate different routines based on different cues. You can put the cheese in a different place and associate it with a bang sound. Then, depending on whether you play a click or a bang, the rat will take the corresponding route.

Interestingly, when the rat's running its routine, its brain goes into autopilot. The rat's brain activity is a lot less active than it is when normally exploring the world. If you've ever zoned out while doing something pretty complex, like backing out of the driveway, you know the feeling.

Understanding the anatomy of a habit allows us to fully appreciate what is required to adopt new habits or eliminate bad ones. It also helps us understand why good habit formation lies at the heart of having a remarkable life. I am convinced good habits lie at the heart of what Jim Collins was referring to about discipline in his quote I have previously shared, "Greatness is not a function of circumstance; greatness, it turns out, is a matter of conscious choice and *discipline*." You see, our great intentions will fail us, and we will fall short on even our deepest commitments, if we haven't created habits and rituals that let us be our best in good times and bad, sickness and health, or triumph and defeat. And the seven habits of this book that I have outlined in the previous chapters have as much science behind them as any other habits. Hopefully, by engaging this book and having the discipline to make these your habits, your life will be even more remarkable.

THE POWER OF RITUAL

As I have shared several times, one of my great heroes is John Bonviaggio. He never got past the fifth grade, but talk about wisdom—he's got it in spades. He would give these magnificent talks. He was a phenomenal husband and father. One time, I did a father-son trip to New York City with my son, Erik, and asked John if he would be our tour guide, not to the famous sites that most tourists go but the sites that John would describe when he would share his experiences of "serving the forlorn of the Bowery," the alcoholics and mentally suffering whom John made it his mission to feed, clothe, and care for.

We were staying with John, and when we were heading back to his house on Staten Island after an incredible day in places like Chinatown, Canal Street, Little Italy, the Bowery, and Greenwich Village, he did something remarkable just before he pulled into his garage. He said, "There's my prayer rock." He indicated that for many years he felt that he always needed a clear way to help him transition from whatever roles and responsibilities he had outside his home, to being husband and father when he pulled his car into his garage. He picked out a stone right outside his house and designated it his "prayer rock" and he would always stop and pray that he could be the man, husband, and father that his family needed him to be. He would pray that God would grant him the compassion and insight to leave work at work and allow him to be loving to, and present with, his family. Erik and I were very moved by John's example, and watching him in action with his family, it was clear his prayer and deep intention were being answered. That prayer was John's habit and ritual. That prayer was part of him being purposeful and mindful. That prayer allowed him to downshift and be intentional about being the best possible husband and father.

We are bombarded by all sorts of things throughout the day—the constant cycle of news, daily events, meetings, requirements, etc. It's hard to be reflective in the midst of very busy, demanding days. It becomes absolutely critical to have an early-morning or late-night ritual where you take time to be clear about what's important and about how you're going to make today or tomorrow count. Or do as John did—pick a transition point that whenever he approached that point, it was the cue that triggered his prayer routine. And because he was then more intentional about positively engaging his family, it gave him a positive feeling and reward, which in turn deepened the habit.

It's a new mental image. In the introduction to one of the longest-running soap operas, "Days of Our Lives," the narrator said these profound words, "Like sand through the hourglass, so are the days of our lives." I don't want to spend a lot of time arguing with others about what our lives look like when we die. What we can all count on is death, and so I am most concerned with how I use this one life I have to its fullest extent. The great news is that barring a car accident or some other catastrophe, as long as I keep taking good care of my mind, heart, and spirit, there's a good chance I'll live to be ninety years old. (A man's life expectancy in America in 2015 was 78.4 years, but there is extremely wide variation due largely to lifestyle and socioeconomic factors.)

I turned 58 last October and if one does the math, I have about 11,700 days to make the most of and relish and enjoy. Seeing as I have already used up 21,320 days, I want to make sure I am making the most of what days I do have. Rather than see that as a morbid thing, it is a reality and a responsibility to make sure we are doing all we can to make this "wild and precious life" as meaningful and positive as possible.

So how do we make sure we're living the life we choose?

I refuse to live out of a space that says, "My life may not have a happy ending." I'm going to do everything I can to have the happiest ending I possibly can. I recite Viktor Frankl at least several times a week. "Everything can be taken from a man but one thing; the last of human freedoms to choose one's attitude in any given set of circumstances, to choose one's own way." Unless something drastic in my life changes, the circumstances of my life have no comparison to the horrific conditions that Frankl survived in the German concentration camps, and therefore, I have no excuse not to choose the most empowering response and attitude I possibly can. I find that enormously empowering. You and I are the chief scriptwriters of our lives and if we don't like where the script is taking us, we have great power to change the script and choose a better path.

It is so much easier to choose a better path by having habits and rituals that support a better path. When I do my early-morning and late-night rituals that include the habits of this book, I am being as intentional as I can about how I want to make this day matter.

SOME TIPS FOR HABIT CREATION

Beyond having those early-morning or late-night rituals to remind you of your purpose and intention, here are some tips to create habits:

1. Find simple cues or triggers. For me, an easy cue is my morning alarm. My alarm goes off and it's my cue to work out. It's not just an alarm, not just an annoying noise to get me out of bed. It's a sound that I've connected to the daily habit of movement. I reinforce that cue with wearing my gym clothes to bed.

2. With any habit you are forming, make sure there is sufficient reward. For me, I exercise because I know there's a positive benefit. I'll write my workout in my gratitude journal, and that's affirming. Also, no matter what else happens that day, I will have accomplished something significant. When I don't exercise in the morning, I'm not as clear thinking and I'm more sluggish.

   Duane didn't get all of these rewards, though, so he had to be more creative. He loves to check off boxes, so when he works out, he gets to check a box. That's a reward. Duane's mother-in-law died in her early sixties from cancer, and they are still reeling from her death. Nothing gives Duane more joy than being a good husband. When he and his wife work out together, it helps their relationship, so that's another reward. He also knows that his wife likes it when he's healthier, so it's all part of a positive cycle.

3. Start small. Don't make the mountain so high that you never begin to climb. Also, be thoughtful and

intentional about understanding that for anything to be a habit, there has to be a cue and a reward. If you want new habits to show up in your life, think like a scientist and ask, "What's going to be my reward for running three miles?" Find a meaningful reward, something you love and enjoy.

4. Also, we need to make this fun. I stumbled upon a game that for a few years really helped me establish and sustain some great habits. Several years ago, I was trying to create better habits in my life, especially around gratitude and positive emotion. I had read somewhere of a person assigning points to good things that happened in their day and I thought I could do the same thing. My goals would be to get 100 points a day, 1,000 points a week, and 5,000 points a month. I gave myself points for various things—ten points for a meaningful workout, ten points for eating well (not overeating) at all three meals, ten points for a great coaching session. If special things happened that were week-worthy, I'd award myself twenty-five points. For example, when my daughter got accepted into a great school, I was so happy for her that I gave myself twenty-five points. If something happened that was month-worthy, such as a client I met with told me that something we had discussed made a huge difference in their life, I would get 100 points. If Claudia and I took a great vacation or if a new client signed a new

contract for 12 months, I might give myself 250 points. At the end of the day when I'd tally my points and I achieved my goal, serotonin and dopamine would flood my brain. I didn't take points away and I didn't assign negative points, by the way. The game also helps all the habits work together. If you're doing all seven habits, that's seventy points. You'd just need 3 other positive things to happen to get to 100! I did this for about three years, and while it took intention and great effort to keep the game going week-in and week-out, it had enormous benefit on me, especially in focusing so much of my days on seeing the good and the realization that you usually find what you are looking for. The game truly helped me see the richness of my life and the enormous opportunities I had every day to be positive and share the positive with others.

5. Getting positive reinforcement for our habits is also key. Duhigg describes in *The Power of Habit* that at the turn of the 20th century, it was estimated that less than 25 percent of Americans brushed their teeth regularly. A brilliant marketer came up with a slogan around the words "minty fresh," for the new toothpaste brand, Pepsodent. People started to make a connection between their mouths needing to be cleaned and the minty fresh taste proving they were clean. After this marketing campaign, parents started buying into the need for daily

hygiene and through their daily reinforcement of brushing with their children, well over 90 percent of Americans were brushing their teeth regularly.

The marketing campaign in the early twentieth century was on erasing the dirty film from our teeth and getting a clean, fresh mouth, and it worked because people were feeling positive about their cleanliness, not bad about their teeth being unclean.

Think about that! This habit is almost uniformly accepted and practiced by the majority of people in the world. What if we could apply similar thinking and habit-forming strategies to something equally important like putting sunscreen on prior to going out into the sun? Daily movement? Calorie consumption moderation?

LETTING YOUR HABITS GROW

William James wrote that all of our life is but a mass of habits.

That's true—but it can be up to us what those habits are.

Begin with one habit. Just one. Then let that show you that you have the capacity to create new habits. It takes intention, science, thoughtfulness, and discipline. But the seven habits focused on in this book are about giving you the capacity and awareness to see yourself as the author of your own life. Be intentional about having a happy ending. See how one good habit can lead to two, can lead to four, can lead to seven.

Chapter 13

ENERGY MANAGEMENT

I attended the concert of world-renowned trumpet player, Chris Botti, at Symphony Hall in Atlanta, and the concert was amazing. As part of his show, Chris had an extraordinary drummer, who played a twelve-minute solo. I was mesmerized by the performance, as the drummer used every single part of his body...for twelve minutes. It was just as athletic as it was artistic. He was sweating profusely as he gave everything he possibly could to his performance solo. Watching him drum, I could only think that this man was a master of energy management.

When I read *The Power of Full Engagement* by Jim Loehr and Tony Schwartz, it was a huge "aha" moment for me when the authors made a simple point: we all have the same amount of time. "Energy, not time, is the fundamental currency of high performance," they write.

What the greatest people in any endeavor have is the capacity to bring greater energy to those moments that really matter. While we can't create more time by being thoughtful, deliberate, and disciplined, we can create more energy. Loehr and Schwartz have studied and coached high-performing athletes and one of their foundational principles for success is how great athletes are as intentional about their rest and recovery as they are about their performance.

In 2001, prior to the release of their book, Loehr and Schwartz wrote an HBR article that had enormous impact on me and I have shared it with as many clients as possible. In "The Making of a Corporate Athlete," they lay out their ideas on energy management and the concept of the *Ideal Performance State* (IPS). The IPS reflects a condition when athletes are able "to bring their talents and skills to full ignition and to sustain high performance over time." The capacity to mobilize energy on demand is the foundation of IPS.

The authors point out that there are two essential components to energy management. The first is the rhythmic movement by the athlete between energy expenditure (stress) and energy renewal (recovery). They found that the real enemy of high performance is not stress but the absence of disciplined, intermittent recovery. And the second component of energy management is the creation of disciplined rituals that promote rhythmic stress and recovery. For me, this concept was blindingly obvious, but clearly not something I had understood and more importantly practiced in my life, especially regarding self-care, rest, and sleep.

The HBR article also made it easy for my clients and me to make the intellectual leap from high-performing athletes to high-performing leaders and executives. And as much as I have discussed the concepts with others, I also continue to find that probably one of the most challenging things for a driven, high-expectation leader is to take appropriate time to rest, relax, recover, and rejuvenate.

Recently, I was with a client who has a very demanding role and over the last eight months has taken a total of four vacation days. I challenged him that taking some well-deserved time off was not only good for his well-being but the well-being of the many people who work for him. I also asked him to consider that he had spent a good portion of his professional life working hard to "save" the world and that as he is in the second half of his life (as am I), perhaps he needed to spend more time learning how to "savor" the world as well.

As I reflect on Chris Botti's amazing drummer, there was no way that he could create what he did for as long as he did with that amount of energy without being intentional about how he recovered and managed his energy. No one can. In fact, the most energetic among us know this well: you can't go 100 percent, 100 percent of the time. You can't push yourself to exhaustion and keep pushing without dire consequences. The best athletes know this, even though, watching them, we might think otherwise. Think about Michael Phelps, for example. He is just as intentional about his recovery as he is about his training. In an article for Men's Fitness about Phelps's training regimen (at peak training he was consuming as much as 10,000 calories a day and swimming about 50 miles a week), it highlights how seriously Phelps took his recovery. "Sleep is also a big part of my recovery," Phelps is quoted saying. "It's really important that my body gets enough rest so that I'm ready to go for my next race or training session."

In Malcolm Gladwell's book *Outliers: The Study of Success*, he says those who are the greatest at any endeavor are the ones who are best at managing their energy so that when they need to perform at their best, they have the energy to do so. One of the greatest tennis players who diminished his capacity for greatness was John McEnroe. If we watched a video of McEnroe and Roger Federer at their best, we would see distinct differences in how each handled themselves in-between volleys. If the judge made a call McEnroe disagreed with, he would frequently become irate and attempt to badger, cajole, and share his rage with the judge. Federer, on the other hand, knows that getting worked up over a bad call is a sure way to drain important energy needed for playing. Federer is referred to as "the iceman" because of how he consistently remains calm, but it's more than that. He wastes as little energy as possible. He knows that you can't give what you don't have.

Federer's accomplishments are extraordinary as he has won an all-time record twenty Grand Slam singles titles, reached a record thirty Grand Slam finals to include a streak of ten consecutive appearances, twenty-three consecutive semifinal appearances, and thirty-six consecutive quarterfinal appearances. If you look at John McEnroe's Wikipedia page, it reads that his accomplishments are: "He went on to win several Grand Slam championships, earning fame for his impressive skills and rivalry with Björn Borg *along with a volatile court persona*." I wonder how much more accomplished McEnroe could have been if he had better managed his energy on the court? And it's sad that his negative court demeanor has remained a big part of his legacy.

THE DANGER OF NOT MANAGING ENERGY

As you think about living a life of meaning and purpose,

rooted in joy, happiness, and resiliency, you need lots of energy to do that. What often happens to marriages over time is that partners stop putting energy into making the relationship as fun as it was when they started dating. You have to be intentional and have energy for that. When we're courting, we're trying to be as creative as possible to win the other over. Over time, we get stale and we're tired. You have to ask yourself: Are you living life? Or is life living you? If you want to have a happy, meaningful marriage or any successful relationship for that matter, you have to invest in it; it won't happen on its own. Just as we saw that energy is the currency of great athletic performance, it too is the currency of relationship building, and of leadership. We fall and stay in love with people, and we follow leaders, because they are energizing, enthusiastic, exciting. We want some of that.

If we don't have it to give, then everything—our relationships, our careers, our parenting, our lives—suffers for it.

When we're exhausted, we're not getting the same level of brain neural activity. We have this magnificent brain that distinguishes us from all other creatures, but it is easily exhausted. We tend to ignore that fact because we can't see it. We tend to think that we have the same mental acuity at 9 a.m. on a Tuesday morning as we do at 5 p.m. on a Friday, when we would describe our week as demanding, stressful, packed, and at times overwhelming.

I had a client coaching session last Friday at four in the afternoon and when I called, the client had just finished four intense days on the road where he was in three different locations dealing with a host of difficult challenges.

I could sense his weariness and frustration and asked him, "On a scale of one to ten, ten being *I could not feel more professionally fulfilled and satisfied* and one being, *I could not feel more professionally dissatisfied*, how would you rate yourself?"

With no hesitation, he said, "Probably a three." And I said, "Do you think you might score yourself differently on Monday morning after you have had some downtime with your family and forget a bit about work?"

He paused and reflected. "Yeah, I probably would rate myself differently but certainly not a ten!"

I responded, "Let's assume it's Monday, you are feeling more refreshed and recovered from the weekend, and let's tackle ways in which you can move closer to that ten."

We need to be honest with ourselves that when we are worn out, there is a high probability we are not doing our best thinking. I always joke with my clients about an Israeli study that was done on parole judges and looking at the quality of their judgments at the beginning of the day and week versus the end of the day and week. The studies show conclusively that, when tired or hungry, judges make different decisions. In particular, when not at their best, they tend to make the least risky judgments and for an inmate looking for parole—that means being denied parole. My joke to clients is, should you find yourself in prison seeking parole, try to get your hearing at the beginning of the day and week!

As I have spoken and written more about the opportunities to better balance our energy expenditures with our energy renewal and recovery, I have found myself being more intentional about striking that balance more thoughtfully, and especially in using the seven habits I have described throughout this book. I don't think I have been busier in my professional and personal life. But I also have never been more productive. Yet, I sustain my capacity to get it all done by being clear in my daily purpose, hunting for the good to cultivate positive emotions as well as expressing gratitude, deepening my relationships with others, being clear about and hopeful for my future, meditating at least ten minutes a day, and exercising. Those things aren't extras; they're essential to me being at my best and achieving my ideal performance state, as described by Loehr and Schwartz.

TAKE A VACATION

One of my clients, a health-care leader with immense responsibilities and high-visibility pressures, had accumulated 400 hours of vacation that she hadn't used. You read that number correctly. If you do the math, that's fifty days of vacation. While the organization she works for is getting an awesome deal since those vacation days are an integral part of her compensation and not being used, it is terribly unfair to her, the people who work for her, and of course, all those in her life who would hopefully spend time with her while on vacation.

I was taken aback by her statement, and she could see the concern on my face. She responded quickly, "My kids came to me the other day and said we don't do anything fun as a family. That's not right, is it?"

My response was hopefully said with as much compassion as possible, "No, it's not right for them and it's not right for you. You work too hard and give too much not to take your vacation. It is something you have earned. Furthermore, I don't think it's healthy for you or for those you lead and serve. What can you do over the next several months to change that?"

To her credit, she made a commitment and over the next thirty days did take a week-long vacation to Disney and came back overjoyed with the experience. She was very excited and proud to share the news with me when we met after the vacation.

As we discussed previously, Americans get the least amount of vacation of any developed country in the world, and what we do get, many of us don't use. From a financial standpoint, that's just giving money back to your employer when you don't use your vacation time, forfeiting well over *$60 billion in benefits.*

But it's much costlier than that. You're hurting your mental, emotional, and physical well-being when you don't take vacation. Numerous studies show that taking vacations reduces stress, decreases the risk of cardiovascular disease, improves sleep patterns, and improves productivity. For example, in one study, women who took a vacation once every six years or less were almost eight times more likely to develop heart disease, have a heart attack, or die of a coronary-related cause than those who took at least two vacations a year. Ernst & Young conducted an internal study of its employees and found that for each additional ten hours of vacation time employees took, their year-end performance ratings improved 8 percent, and frequent vacationers were significantly less likely to leave the firm.

Human beings are not meant to be on, 24/7. In Japan, there is an epidemic of overwork. Not too long ago, there was a news report of a woman in Japan who died from overwork after logging 159 hours of overtime in the month leading up to her death. The woman suffered from heart failure, but officials in Tokyo deemed the thirty-one-year-old had died from *karoshi*—death from overwork—after taking just two days off in the sixty days before she died, according to *The Japan Times*. The rest of Japan could learn from its island of Okinawa, where the people live very differently, culturally, than the people in big cities like Tokyo and Kyoto.

In America, many of us work jobs that are high-pressure, high-responsibility, and long hours. In order to be successful, you have to work longer and harder, and you get into a grind you can't see your way out of. If you take a vacation, you start to think about all the things that will go undone and the 1,000 emails you'll have when you get back and it starts to feel not even worth it to take a vacation. I call it the downward spiral. The research is clear that the more you work without adequate recovery, the less effective you become. I believe that part of why people are working longer is because they don't have the energy to be at their best when they are working. You're less effective, requiring you to work longer and harder without a break.

That creates issues for people who aren't healthy physically, mentally, emotionally, or spiritually. Thankfully, leaders and organizations are starting to notice this, seeing its lethal effects on the engagement and productivity of their workforce and taking better steps to create work environments, as well as expectations and incentives that motivate, inspire, educate, and direct better self-care to include people taking vacations and engaging in more activities dedicated to movement, mindfulness, and community building and sharing.

YES, YOU NEED SLEEP

I know these issues as well as anyone. I used to wear my exhaustion as a badge of honor. My wife and I haven't fought much over the years about the typical marriage issues such as money and children; instead, we used to fight about sleep. My wife loves a great nap, and she could probably count on one hand how many naps I've taken in our married life. Despite a course I took at Harvard on sleep deprivation back in 1989, I held on to a terribly misguided belief that strong people need less sleep. For well over twenty-six years, I'd start out on Sunday getting maybe five to six hours of sleep, then on Monday a little less, then Tuesday a little less and so on until Friday rolled around and I'd be barely holding on because I was so tired. On the weekends, when I should have been at my best for my wife and my children, I was at my worst because I was exhausted. I have no idea how many years I took off my life from that crazy mindset. It's not something I'm proud of.

It wasn't until I read *The Power of Full Engagement* that I finally understood energy management versus time management, and the vital importance of sufficient sleep on being at my best and most ideal performance state. I have to admit I can be really slow to grasp important things and I am grateful that I had a "wake-up" call from my terrible sleeping habits and realized that if I did not change, I was not only taking years off my life but I was not making the most of the life I had. From that moment on, I have been religious about making sure I get seven to seven and a half hours of sleep each night. I track my sleep through my Fitbit so I know when I'm restless or wake up in the night. When I realize I'm under seven hours of productive sleep, I'll schedule myself for eight hours or more of sleep the next night to catch up and revitalize myself.

That book was life-changing, and I am grateful for the changes that it prompted me to take. It allowed me to finally understand that by managing my energy—taking better care of myself and my relationships, being more organized and prepared mentally, and starting each day with purpose (spiritual alignment)—I would be able to have a happy ending. By investing in the four domains of the pyramid of full engagement, I have so much more energy to do the work I do and give to the people I serve.

CHILL OUT

I had previously shared the story of my emotional and heated argument with my dear friend, Mike, over Labor Day regarding some volatile healthcare issues. And how I was most fortunate to have this out-of-body experience of watching myself begin to babble, as my emotions began to grab hold of my ability to articulate my point of view with some clarity and eloquence. What was insightful about this experience is that because I was able to "get on the balcony" to observe myself spin out of control, I was in turn able to quickly get back into control. That incident is a reminder of how important it is to find pockets of respite and "chill" throughout our long and challenging days to not only sustain us but to help us see and speak so much more clearly. One of my clients happily declared her theme this year to be the year of "The Pause" and as she reminded herself daily of her theme, it was a way to strengthen her ability to slow down, breathe, reflect more, and then, only then, respond. I have not heard how it is working for her, but I am very confident that her theme will serve her well.

ENERGY AND THE SEVEN HABITS

Better managing our energy is paramount to building the seven habits, and the seven habits are paramount to increasing our ability to manage our energy. It is an upward spiral that I have come to deeply believe will help us have even more remarkable and full lives.

Creating new habits to replace old habits is heavy lifting. It is why New Year's resolutions fail. Old habits are these deeply carved ruts in our brains. To bring about a new habit requires tremendous physical, emotional, and mental acuity. Energy management is the mechanism, the levers, to make it happen. This is why, hopefully years from now we'll be teaching elementary students how to meditate along with most companies looking to improve their employee engagement, creativity, and productivity. The research is so abundantly clear that having your mind be at rest strengthens its future capacity to think. As we all know, it is far better for us to be in control of our thoughts rather than our thoughts controlling us.

The seven habits help maximize energy management and vice versa.

We underestimate how hard it is to sustain habits because we overestimate the difficulty of even getting started. You can make it easy to get started by finding small steps you can take toward each of the seven habits. Remember our example from our chapter on movement, with the woman who quit smoking by taking the small step of running around her block. That gave her something to build upon until she finally quit smoking and became a runner.

My meditation practice is filled with hundreds of failures. But that's okay! We just get back up and start again. No one is keeping score for you. Let the failures go and get back on the horse.

As I write this, I am grateful that today I hit nine days of meditation in a row. This is a personal best and this morning when I finished my meditation and looked at my Calm app, it showed the month with the nine days in a row of meditation and it felt really great. Additionally, it increased my motivation to work harder at sustaining the habit and I can't wait to do it again tomorrow. I am reminded that one of my clients, to whom I had suggested that she start a meditation practice, told me last month that she had established a streak of twenty-four days, and frankly her example motivated me to get even more habitual about my meditation practice—and I have! I am grateful for her and I will make sure I share that with her when we are together again.

PLANNING YOUR ENERGY

Given the vital role that energy management plays in our lives, we must be more intentional about planning those rhythmic cycles of energy expenditure and energy renewal. Some of us are good at planning our days, ensuring that all of our priorities and tasks we are responsible for get scheduled, but most of us don't plan out how we are using and recovering our energy. So many of my clients pack their days beginning at 7 a.m., and sometimes starting even at 6 a.m. and stretching well until early evening, with meetings frequently back to back and not even allowing for the opportunity to eat lunch and waiting until they get home late to have dinner.

Just yesterday, a client was sharing that they overheard a group of operating nurses sharing that the surgeons they worked with, and deeply respected, had so many cases that they were not taking breaks. They weren't even eating breakfast or lunch. Unfortunately, the nurses could see that not taking breaks or eating took a toll on the emotional and energy management of their surgeons as they got, in their words, "hangry" and more critical, impatient, and sarcastic as the day wore on. If you were to interview hospital staff across the country who work in operating rooms, you would find many similar stories. It doesn't have to be this way. We know we need to eat throughout the day. We know we need to take breaks and we know that like great athletes, we cannot keep going with the same intensity, focus, and clarity without balancing the work with some rest and recovery.

So be intentional about how you spend your day. To make my day as meaningful as possible, I need to be as engaging and purposeful at my first meeting at 8 a.m. as I am when I engage a client for dinner at 6 p.m. The only way to be at your best throughout the day is to manage your energy.

You must remember that you have the control to change

these things. You do. It might feel like you don't, because you're used to your job or your life being a certain way—we acclimate to the culture of our lives. But we can change it. Imagine, for a moment, what your ideal day would look like, how you might manage that energy so you have so much more to give. Seems nice, doesn't it?

Make it happen.

============= *Chapter 14* =============

SUPPORT AND ACCOUNTABILITY

Many of you are likely familiar with dieting...and failed dieting. Diets are very hard to sustain. Jean Nidetch had struggled trying to stay at a healthy weight. She kept failing. She created Weight Watchers after wondering what it would look like to engage a circle of like-minded friends who could be part of her accountability group.

What would it look like if she made a public commitment to lose a certain amount of weight? Weight reduction can be simple math; the more calories you consume above what you're burning comes with a high probability that you'll gain weight. The opposite is also true. If you use more calories than you consume, science says you should lose weight.

The math is easy, but doing it is hard.

And doing it alone is even harder.

That is why people in Weight Watchers keep records of weight loss and share those records with each other. They are held publicly accountable at weekly weigh-ins. When a member loses weight, they all celebrate, encouraging them to continue the journey. Taking this approach wasn't rocket science, but it was brilliant because of how it allowed people to build and sustain a habit of weight loss. The math didn't change. The support did.

Or take something that can be even harder than weight loss: kicking a substance addiction. Clearly, an alcoholic has an addiction. There is a cue to begin drinking and the reward is the feeling that comes from drinking. That reward becomes so strong that our brain wants more of it and begins to convince us that we cannot do without it. To break this deeply ingrained habit by ourselves is so incredibly difficult.

I was reading a very sad story recently about a former vice chairman of the Joint Chiefs of Staff, a four-star admiral by the name of James Winnefeld, and how his youngest son died of a terrible overdose of opioids. The admiral and his wife had helped their son go through what they thought was a very successful rehab experience and they were so confident of his progress that they agreed he would attend a university in Denver. The son was a paramedic and taking a class in a part of town where there was easy access to drug users and suppliers. Despite the son's knowledge and experience, just being in close proximity to what he once knew and craved, he relapsed and regrettably, it was lethal.

As recent reports indicate that close to ninety-four Americans are dying each day of opioid and heroin overdoses, unless America takes drastic action, this will be an epidemic of gigantic proportions.

One of my uncles, Fr. Edwin Coyne, lived an extraordinary life, yet openly described himself as an alcoholic for a good portion of his life. He claimed alcoholism as his disease and yet was sober since 1939 and had an amazing career as a Roman Catholic priest serving in the poorest of communities in the Diocese of Bridgeport, Connecticut, as well as serving the indigenous people of the Andes Mountains in South America. He liked to call himself a "street priest" because for him that is where he saw his ministry and where he really found God.

While he proudly claimed that God saved him, it was Alcoholics Anonymous (AA) that was his lifeline. While Fr. Ed passed away several years ago, up until he was no longer mobile, he would attend three to four AA meetings a week and had done that religiously since becoming sober. I had the privilege of attending with many of my family, Fr. Ed's thirty-fifth celebration of his priesthood, and I was amazed that there was a slew of his friends that our family had no connection to or knowledge of. They were his AA community, as well as representatives from Russia AA, as it turns out that my uncle was one of the first to bring the gift of AA to the Soviet Union (completely unbeknownst to our family!). Besides Fr. Ed, I have known quite a few friends who were saved by AA, and I think the program deserves further explanation given this book's purpose and point of view.

The Alcoholics Anonymous co-founder, Bill Wilson, had no formal science degrees. What he had through his own tormented journey with fighting alcoholism was a notion that you needed to find a way for people to replace their addiction to alcohol with an addiction to something else equally as powerful. Furthermore, he knew that getting free of addiction required a deep commitment, and intention to live a better way with a structure to keep them focused, disciplined, and habitual in the same ways that their alcoholism was habitual.

Bill Wilson believed that if he could get social support to become the alcoholic's habit instead of drinking, AA could save lives.

One of the most important pieces of AA is that when you sign up, you're given a sponsor, a real human being who you are encouraged to call anytime for support. Your sponsor is a recovering alcoholic, who has walked in your shoes and has a mission to help you build the habit of following the process of AA. There is a twelve-step process. One of the first things you're taught is that instead of having a drink, call your sponsor.

They also try to get you to ninety meetings in ninety days. While Bill may not have studied much science, he certainly knew the underpinnings of creating habits. There are over 100,000 registered locations for AA members to gather, and AA works hard at making it easy for you to become hooked on meetings instead of booze.

While AA does not work for everyone, it has had enormous impact, helping many alcoholics recover and all the residual positive effect that has on families and societies. Three days before Fr. Ed went to the hospital (where he died approximately a week later), he was at an AA meeting. He was addicted to AA and was deeply grateful for its positive impact on his life and the lives of so many others he knew.

THE STRENGTH OF SUPPORT

In the book, *The Influencer: The New Science of Leading*

Change by Joseph Grenny, Kerry Patterson, David Maxfield, Ron McMillan, and Al Switzler, there is a delightful story about the Atlanta-based Carter Center and its commitment to eradicate guinea worm in the world. In 1986, the disease afflicted an estimated 3.5 million people a year in 21 countries in Africa and Asia. Today, thanks to the work of the Carter Center and its partners that include every country affected, the incidence of guinea worm has been reduced by more than 99.99 percent to just 30 cases in 2017.

The story centers on how the Carter Center's strategy, called the Guinea Worm Eradication Program, focused on high community engagement interventions to include targeted education and change behavior, such as teaching communities to filter all drinking water and preventing transmission of the worm by keeping anyone with an emerging worm from entering the community's water sources. They also provided cheap but highly effective water filters so that every person accessing the water supply had one and were taught how to boil the water, too. And when a villager played a part in keeping someone from using a contaminated water source without precautions, they received and got to wear a T-shirt that said they played a significant part of Guinea Worm Eradication.

As with AA and Weight Watchers, social support done right really works. The T-shirts worn in the villages that are eradicating Guinea Worm have become highly coveted. Isn't that amazing to think that a T-shirt can actually be a tool for change? In this case, a medical tool? The filters were necessary, of course, but what makes those filters have their full impact is that they became entwined with the community. People were looking out for each other, offering support by teaching and keeping everyone accountable by checking each other's water sources.

Accountability and social support work together. Accountability improves discipline. When we publicly share whatever it is we've committed to—weight loss, listening better, quitting smoking, etc.—we allow people to actively give us feedback about how well we're doing living up to our commitment and it creates accountability. If I don't show up to my CrossFit class at six like usual, my CrossFit gang will ask me about it.

I often remind clients that life is a team sport and despite me having the privilege of going to a great institution like West Point and being a part of some of the finest infantry units in the US Army, and working at extraordinary places like McKinsey and Company, or attending Harvard Business School, for so many years, I hid my deep insecurities from others and rarely if ever asked for help and guidance. It has taken me a long, long time to have the courage to ask others for help and to "put myself out there" for others to give me feedback, offer perspective, and help me be my best self. Gratefully, so many friends and family have been willing to help me be a better man.

MOTIVATION FROM THE OUTSIDE

We all need greater motivation—and support fuels motivation.

Just think if we all worked more to motivate and help each other be our best. Forty percent of American adults are obese, and that number grows each year. Alarmingly, 60 percent of cancers in our country are diagnosed in people who are obese.

If we had more support and accountability, would America get healthier?

One of my clients has had great success in helping patients better manage their hypertension (high blood pressure) by putting them in a cohort that also involved the patients' spouses and family members. A key hypertension reduction strategy is to get patients to lower the salt content in their food. There is a reason that some of the unhealthiest people in our country live in places where the food is plentiful, rich, and laden with lots of sugar and salt. Lowering salt content is not an easy thing to do unless you can make a compelling case to the whole family for change and make sure they are part of the change effort.

By bringing their spouses into the plan, especially if the spouse does the cooking, they get involved with helping their loved one achieve an optimal level of blood pressure. This cohort has been highly successful because of the community of support and accountability.

SUPPORT AND RESILIENCE

Social support also improves resilience. Remember Sebastian Junger's *Tribe: On Homecoming and Belonging*, where some returning veterans experienced prolonged PTSD not because of the terrors they experienced in battle but because they lost their social bonds when they left the war? When you lose your social bonds with others and become isolated, it is much easier to lose your resiliency, your capacity to bounce back from difficulty and challenge.

Martin Seligman, in the program he sold and delivered to the US Army on resiliency, taught that strong connections with others was one of six core competencies of resilience besides: optimism, character strengths, mental agility, self-awareness, and self-regulation. And within the competency of connections, Seligman lists these several core components:

- Strong relationships
- Positive and effective communication
- Empathy

- Willingness to ask for help
- Supporting others

As I look at the list, I find it to be quite consistent with my own experience. It affirms what I have written earlier about the willingness to ask for help, supporting others, and empathy.

When you are with people who are positive and who care about, support, and value you, it helps you keep going in the face of difficulty.

As we also know from the Blue Zones, three of the "Power Nine" elements have to do with strong social bonds with one's family, one's friends, and one's tribe or community. I have seen studies that show that the more friends and love in one's life, the less illness, and that people who have at least one friend they would be comfortable calling at three in the morning to tell their troubles to, were healthier. Happy people usually have richer social networks than unhappy people, and social connectedness contributes to a lack of disability as we age. Somewhere along my journey I have come to see that while misery may love company, company does not love misery and miserable people tend to repel other people, leading to even more loneliness, pessimism, and unhappiness.

Accountability and social support are two sides of the

same coin for effective habit creation. Social support gives us the positive emotions of encouragement, and accountability is us not wanting to let people down and living up to our commitments and promises.

THE DANGER OF ISOLATION

Change in isolation is hard. Our brains get tired easily. Our willpower waxes and wanes. It's the support and accountability that provides the extra motivation needed to sustain meaningful habits like the seven I have described in detail in this book that I believe support having a remarkable life.

America has a significant problem with physician and nurse burnout. I sat on a panel with a physician who was tasked with combating burnout at the Mayo Clinic. One of the main things they are doing is giving physicians time to gather in small groups in intimate settings and talk about their challenges while receiving support and affirmation from their colleagues. When you can provide that kind of time and care, it helps prevent burnout and build resiliency.

Doctors who don't seek social support often get cynical, angry, or sarcastic, and there's more burnout. According to a massive study published late last year in the *Journal of the American Medical Association*, a staggering 29 percent of young doctors struggle with depression. The authors of that study also cite causes ranging from workload and sleep deprivation to bullying by other doctors and a culture that stigmatizes mental health treatment.

A 2015 study by Mayo Clinic on the prevalence of physician burnout reported that almost 55 percent of the physicians who participated in the study reported at least one symptom of burnout. It is a significant problem in America's hospitals and thankfully, many organizations like the Mayo Clinic are actively taking steps to better understand it and treat it in more comprehensive ways.

Burnout isn't just feeling a loss of control. It's hopelessness. As you go down the path of burnout, you tend to pull away, isolating yourself. One of the ways you isolate yourself is being more sarcastic, bitter, and frustrated. People don't like being around you. It just creates a downward spiral.

As I talk to healthcare leaders across the country about burnout, I challenge them to ask how they can take care of their own. One way is to make sure no one is an island well before anyone gets burned out. Colleagues should care about each other enough to notice and say something when one seems down and is pulling away from the others.

Yet, we underestimate how asking for social support helps us improve. We're not taught to ask for help. Men especially struggle with asking for help. There's a tendency to think that if we ask for help, we're weak, or we'll be perceived as not capable. On the flip side, we love giving help! It gives me great joy, in fact, to help someone else. We underestimate that when we ask for help, we're giving someone else the opportunity to be of service, and that's important.

OPENING UP

Harvard Business School started an initiative several years ago where alumni groups across the country were formed with the purpose of providing a safe and confidential space for approximately ten to twelve alumni to gather monthly to share their struggles, opportunities, concerns, and deepest fears. Recently, I joined such a group in Atlanta and while I am only into our fifth month of gathering, I have found the opportunity to openly share myself with ten other thoughtful and supportive human beings to be a very positive and meaningful experience. I am confident that as I keep showing up and revealing myself, being authentic and engaging my colleagues in the ups and downs of our lives, it will yield great rewards for me and those in my group. I also know that in doing so, I am certainly reinforcing my third habit of deepening my social bonds with others. The experience is also opening me up to feeling not only more connected to others but appreciative and grateful that I have this monthly opportunity.

I have had the privilege of providing over 1,700 leadership assessments and feedback to the client leaders I have served over the years. As we go through their results of what those around them think of their leadership, I always tell these leaders, "You will get the greatest return on investment not because of the dialogue we're having about your assessment but because of the dialogue you can have with the people who took the time to give you meaningful feedback."

One of the greatest things they can do is truly engage the people who gave them the feedback. First, I ask them to thank them for taking the time to invest in their growth and development. Second, I ask them to offer some insight into how that feedback will help them be a better leader. Finally, I suggest to them that they ask their colleagues for their continued help and if it would be okay to check in with them from time to time to see how they're viewing their progress. I cannot recall when a client who followed my suggestions had colleagues who did not respond positively and enthusiastically to being asked for help, support, and continued insight. And not surprisingly, when colleagues see this aggressive follow-up after an assessment, their perceptions of the rated leader's growth and development go up immeasurably.

There is something profound about being vulnerable by opening yourself up and allowing yourself to be real.

When you lower your guard, and allow people to see your humanness, it gives them permission to be more authentic with you as well.

I asked one of my clients recently about the hardest thing she's had to overcome. Without hesitation, she told me about her grandfather, with whom she was very close. He died two months after she got married. Her father, who was only fifty-seven, died two months after that. If it weren't for her faith and the support of dear friends, she doesn't know how she would have gotten through it. She says her drive to be better comes from losing such important people. "I want to live a good life to honor what they were to me. I want to be a good leader. I want to make a difference in people I serve and only wish my father and grandfather could see what I have accomplished. I think they would be proud of me."

When she shared that touching story with me, it brought our relationship to a different level. I saw my client in such a different light. I connected to her story and her humanness regarding her loss as well as her commitment to be the kind of person and leader that her father and grandfather would be proud of. The nature of your connection to another person changes when you know their story. She had lost two people in her life, but by opening up, she gained that much more support from our deepening friendship.

When I talk to large groups, I try to share some of the things I've overcome and my own insecurities. When I was seven or eight, I started to believe the lie that I wasn't enough. Because that voice played a significant role in my early life, it motivated me to always be right. If I was right, maybe then I'd be enough. Just by sharing that one detail, I've let people know it's okay for them to share their own insecurities. They see this guy who went to West Point and has an MBA from Harvard who didn't feel like he was enough. They know they're not alone with their insecurities and they start to feel brave enough to talk about their own experiences.

One of my other partners in leadership*Forward*, Rebecca Henson, has been a wonderful colleague and friend through the almost fifteen years we have worked together. One encounter particularly stands out that will make me forever grateful to Rebecca.

Approximately thirteen years ago, I received some tough feedback about my leadership. Several of those I worked with rated me as narrow-minded, stubborn, and a poor listener. These were things I tried hard to avoid, and so I was disturbed by the feedback. I sought Rebecca out and asked her to provide me with as open and candid feedback as possible of what she experienced with me that might come across as rigid. She thoughtfully considered my request and then shared this insight: "Greg, there are times when you think you are so right about something and will get very passionate about it. To me, when you get like that, it feels like I have to do combat with you, and most days, I just don't have it in me to do that."

I was stunned by the feedback because I knew she was right and that it was something I really needed to change. That feedback was a great gift and it caused me to look hard at how much my identity had been tied to "being right." I would like to think I have made much progress in letting that identity go, but I also know there are times when it rears its ugly head and I can only hope to have the energy to hit my own "pause" button before I injure an important relationship.

SUPPORT IS SOCIAL

Remember what your parents taught you long ago: "you are known by the company you keep"? It's true. Be intentional about the support you seek and the bonds you form. Find people who are going to make you better. We only have so much time. If you have people who want you to hang out in the gutter with them, find some different friends.

There's synergy in the seven habits. Men have fewer friends than women. So many people invest themselves in work and before they know it, their kids are grown, and they look around and they're lonely. There are a lot of people living in loveless marriages, and a lot of people who don't have a lot of friends.

One of the great things about creating habits and getting others to do them with you is you make friends. So, if you want to increase your capacity to have a remarkable life, make life a team sport, not a solo endeavor. This works with anything, not just weight loss or alcoholism or keeping a gratitude journal. Every habit is better sustained and more beneficial when a group is engaged and holding each other accountable, but also when they're encouraging and supporting each other.

The more positive influence you have, the better.

CONCLUSION

If you had the persistence to get to this point in the book, I hope you are ready to rewrite some new things into your life to make it the most remarkable and joyful life possible.

After twenty years of coaching, I have found that the clients who have gotten the most out of coaching are those who are "unbaked." These are the clients who are clear on the things they want to change, believe they can and should change, and are seeking change that is consistent with their values. They also possess a deep humility that helps them be totally open to embracing their shortcomings so that they are in turn open to new growth and improvement.

WRITE YOUR OWN STORY—AND MAKE IT GOOD

If you want to have the most remarkable and significant

life possible, where are the greatest opportunities that will allow you to be your best self? Would your life be worthy of a movie that anyone would be willing to watch?

Because *Blue Like Jazz* by best-selling author Donald Miller became an overnight success, some screenwriters thought his story would make a great movie. In a later book by Miller, *A Million Miles in a Thousand Years: What I Learned by Editing My Life*, he describes how the screenwriters showed up at his door, moved in with him and started looking closely at his life. It wasn't long before they and Miller realized that his life was pretty dull and certainly would not make for a compelling movie.

The book chronicles what Miller does to create a more meaningful and remarkable life. In one chapter, Miller shares that his father had abandoned his family when Miller was very young and when the screenwriters asked about "the rest of the story," Miller indicated there wasn't one, as he had no idea where his father was or what became of him. The screenwriters talked about him being their protagonist. To make the script engaging and the movie worth watching, there's got to be some drama, some obstacle to overcome or adversary to be vanquished. "Let's go find your father," they said. And they did. The journey was exciting, and there was meaningful resolution to the question of what had become of his father.

Miller also realized he was terribly overweight and out of shape. That did not make for a great story, so Miller decided he would start long-distance biking and volunteered for a coast-to-coast bike ride to raise money for Multiple Sclerosis. The book beautifully describes Miller's transformation, not just physically but emotionally and spiritually, as he not only gets in better shape but comes to bond with his fellow riders while doing something worthwhile for a very meaningful purpose.

I was moved by the book, and it prompted me to reflect on my own life. For me, it's not about having a life that is worthy of some screenplay and movie, but it is about having a life that is as full as possible, one in which I use as much of my potential as possible, one in which I made a positive difference in this world, gave more than I took, loved more than I received, and left a legacy of significance that my loved ones would cherish well after I was gone. As I reflected, I realized I had, like Miller, some major work to do. What is the work that you have to do? Are you ready to get moving?

The lesson here is that Miller got moving. He looked at the things that were troubling in his life, even if they weren't obvious, and went after them. He found his father. He got in shape. He met amazing people. He helped raise significant money for a worthy cause. His very memories are worthy of a movie—and he alone gets to live the real version.

His story reminds me once again of Mary Oliver's call to action quote: "What is it you plan to do with your one wild and precious life?"

We are authors of our own story. This is powerful. Remember it. When we see ourselves as the chief author, we stop being victims. We see that we do have a choice in creating a better life. It requires work, lots of work, but we each have the capacity to do it. See yourself as unbaked. Be clear in what you want to change and improve. Create the habits necessary to make your life remarkable. People with meaningful purpose in their lives live longer because they have something to live for. People who are more positive tend to be happier and healthier. People who have strong social, family, and communal connections and relationships have more remarkable lives. Living in a state of gratefulness and sharing it with others is shown to create more joy in our lives. Reflecting on the life you want to live in very clear and vivid detail is shown to greatly increase the probability of this life coming to fruition. Mindfulness and movement both contribute to not only healthy minds and bodies, but create greater conditions for resiliency as well as more joy and happiness.

It is doubtful that I have told you anything in this book that is radically novel or new. If anything, I have provided meaningful examples as well as research and evidence to affirm and confirm what you already knew. Most of

America does not have a "knowing" problem regarding the qualities and elements that contribute to a remarkable life. We have a "doing" problem. Creating new habits is the very best possible way to help you hardwire what you know into what you do all the time.

If you don't like your story, change it. Rewrite it. Start a new chapter. It's *your* story.

HAVE THE RIGHT MINDSET

Stanford psychologist and professor Carol Dweck in her book *Mindset* says there are two kinds of people—those who believe their lot in life is fixed, or as Popeye the cartoon character likes to say, "I am what I am" and so why waste time and effort in trying to change something that is unchangeable; and those who have a growth mindset and believe that each day is an opportunity to get better and improve the quality of our lives.

Basketball great Michael Jordan embodies the growth mindset best in his quote, "I've missed more than 9,000 shots in my career. I've lost almost 300 games. Twenty-six times I've been trusted to take the game-winning shot and missed. I've failed over and over and over again in my life, and that is why I succeed."

Jordan went onto the basketball court each time he played

with a belief that he could get better. He strove to meld his talent with his drive to be great. Every day was an opportunity for him, despite whatever setback may have happened. He decided he would not be defined by the shots he missed but by how hard he worked. That's how he chose to see things.

We are wired for efficiency and to take the path of least resistance. We underestimate how much our mind is always thinking about how to conserve energy. It's more efficient for our brain to keep thinking what it's always been thinking, even when we're wrong. We develop mental models and filters so we can be efficient. A growth mindset takes a lot of energy. A lot of people this morning would have chosen to go back to bed.

Since I started my gratitude exercise, my brain is always seeking things to be grateful for. This book is about hard-wiring evidence-based habits into your life so that you are able to make the best possible choices in your life and be happier, more joyful, and resilient. My gratitude habit is a perfect example of that. It's wired in me now to deliberately hunt for things to be grateful for. And, everywhere I look, I find blessings and gifts to appreciate and savor.

Three weeks ago, my daughter asked if I would go to my granddaughter Estelle's nursery school and perform for approximately eighty children between the ages of two and five. My polished repertoire consisted of, "Head, Shoulders, Knees and Toes," "Hokey-Pokey," and "If You're Happy and You Know it." As Estelle saw me in the gym where I was to perform, she came running over with a big smile and gave me a great hug. I pulled out my iPhone and took her picture. Later, after my amazing performance where Estelle assisted me by dancing next to me while I played and sang, I opened up my Gratitude 365 app and posted the picture of Estelle. Just writing this paragraph and seeing that picture in my mind's eye is life-giving.

For some crazy reason, I keep a few key images, quotes, and stories in my short-term memory and refer to them many times in any given week. (I apologize to my readers since this book has probably dug up too many of those same quotes, images, and stories to illustrate my points.) One of the images I reflect on most frequently is that of a Far Side comic by Gary Larsen that shows a man in hell, fire all around him, toiling away by shoveling coal into a wheelbarrow. What is prominent is that the man has a big, bright grin on his face; it is clear he is whistling some happy song and I always imagine that the song he is whistling is that over-the-top Disney tune from "Song of the South," called "Zip-A-Dee-Doo-Dah" with the man in Hell whistling the tune: "Zip-A-Dee-Doo-Dah, Zip-A-Dee-A, My oh my, what a wonderful day. Plenty of sunshine heading my way, Zip-A-Dee-Doo-Dah. Zip-A-Dee-A."

Looking at the happy, whistling man is the devil (he's got the pitchfork and accompanying horns) standing next to another man and the bubble over his head says, "Somehow, we're just not reaching that guy." For inexplicable reasons, I really love that line. Certainly, I don't find that my life is even remotely anything like hell. Perhaps it is because when I pick up a newspaper or turn on the news, it is so easy to be discouraged and even angered by some of the insanity we are witness to and yet the Far Side comic is a reminder that I have a choice in my attitude as Viktor Frankl wrote, "regardless of circumstance." And that despite whatever storms, difficulties, and challenges come my way, I can refuse to let the world reach me and instead choose joy, happiness, and resilience and share it with as many others as possible.

WHAT'S YOUR STATUE?

A client of mine is an internal medicine doctor, a physician leader, and classical pianist. He has a master's degree in classical piano. I asked him not long ago, "How much joy does playing the piano give you?" He said: "Immense." Yet, it had been several months since he had played. I suggested to him that playing the piano might be a means for him to not only find more joy in life but also to inoculate himself against some of the challenges and demands of his role. I hope he finds the time to play.

Wouldn't we all want the energy and drive that Michelangelo had in 1564 when at eighty-eight he was carving away at another masterpiece? He had a deep sense of meaning about his job—to chip and chisel and paint, to create the magnificent statues of David, the Pieta, and Moses, or the extraordinary paintings in the Sistine Chapel. Be clear in your purpose. Make your life as positive as possible. Just recently I read that one of Michelangelo's first masterpieces was "The Torment of St. Anthony" that he painted at the age of twelve! Michelangelo was creating art for seventy-six years, and I have to believe that there was a deep, creative purpose within Michelangelo that allowed him to live three times as long as his contemporaries.

I read recently in an Oregon State University study that the day a man retires, his mortality risk goes up, while those who work just a year past retirement eligibility lower their risk of premature death by 11 percent. Perhaps one of the best things that kept Michelangelo alive for so long is he did not have a conception of the word, retirement.

Nobody gets through life unbroken. We all face trials and tribulations. Some of us face more than our fair share. Most of us have heard of the movie "Unbroken," directed by Angelina Jolie that came from the book of the same name by Lauren Hillenbrand. It's about Louis Zamperini, who at a young age started getting into trouble but through the care of his older brother, Rick, was saved by track. Louie could run like the wind and in the mid-1930s was one of the best milers in the country. He was unable to make the 1936 US Olympics Team for the 1,500 meters but was able to secure a place on the team for the 5,000 meters.

With only a few months to prepare for the 5,000 meters, he competed in the Olympics and came in eighth. He didn't pace himself well enough; he had too much left toward the end of the race. However, Adolf Hitler noticed his fast finish and asked to meet with him. The 1940s Olympics didn't happen because of the war and he became a bombardier on a B24. At the Battle of Midway, their plane was shot over 750 times, but they landed safely. Several of the crew were killed while Louie, the pilot, Lt. Russel Allen Phillips, and another member survived.

The next day, Lt. Phillips and Louie took on another crew and went to look for a downed aircraft that had landed somewhere in the Pacific. The aircraft they took had severe mechanical malfunctions and they themselves crash landed. Only Louie, Lt. Phillips, and a sergeant survived the crash.

For the next forty-eight days in a life raft, drifting in the hot, torrid sun, they were shot at by passing Japanese fighter aircraft, survived shark attacks, and sustained themselves on nothing but some rain water and a small bird. The sergeant died, probably due to a broken will and a sense of hopelessness. Finally, Louie and Lt. Phillips were rescued—by the Japanese—1,000 miles from where they crash landed. The Japanese imprisoned them. Louie was tortured and brutalized for the next three years by a sadistic guard, nicknamed "the Bird." Yet, Louie endured and was finally liberated when Japan surrendered. The military gave him back-pay for all the time he was imprisoned and thanked him for his service. With no counseling to deal with his severe PTSD that included nightmares of reliving his torture and suffering, Louie found solace in alcohol, and despite finding and marrying a supportive and loving wife, became an out-of-control alcoholic.

In 1949, in desperation and at the encouragement of his wife, Louie attended a Billy Graham revival, found religion and from that day on, never touched a drop of alcohol again. His nightmares ceased, he forgave his captors, and as a Christian evangelist, Louie went on to live an even more remarkable life. One of his recurring themes was forgiveness, and he visited many of the guards from his POW days to let them know that he had forgiven them. This included an October 1950 visit to Sugamo Prison in Tokyo, where many war criminals were imprisoned, and he expressed his forgiveness to them for what they had done. At the winter Olympics in Nagano, Japan, in 1998, he carried the torch; videos of the event show a smiling, waving Louie Zamperini, unbroken, positive, and perhaps even stronger for what he endured and overcame. He even tried to reconcile with the torturer, who unfortunately refused to see him.

I share Louie's amazing journey of resilience because he embodies the story of how even when beset by tragedy, immense suffering, and difficulty, a person through choice, determination, and discipline can create a new story. Certainly, Louie embodies that latter part of Hemingway's quote about overcoming brokenness. Louie lived to the ripe old age of ninety-seven but missed seeing the release of the movie, "Unbroken" by just six months.

I heard Louie speak when he was ninety-three at an event in Atlanta. I left inspired and thinking, "If that man, who experienced so much pain and suffering, can be so positive and remarkable, why can't I?"

Or I might ask myself: "What's the statue I'm carving?"

THE HABITS AND YOUR STORY

How do the seven habits launch us into a more satisfying life story?

Don't we all want to be happier? More joyful? More resilient? Begin with the end in mind. If those are the outcomes you want, this book provides a recipe backed by tremendous amounts of research. Make these habits an integral part of your life and they become woven into the fabric.

These seven habits ensure we're being intentional about filling our lives with happiness, joy, and goodness, and protecting us against the storms that all humans face. You will lose people you love. You will mourn and grieve. The seven habits are ways to deepen your capacity to come back from tragedy, weather any storm, and still find ways to be happy, to smile, to be compassionate, and purposeful.

When I gave my talk on happiness at my church several years ago, I was deeply moved by the imaginary conversations Viktor Frankl would have with his wife as he was marched each morning by gunpoint. Here was a guy who had no idea if his family was still alive. He was marched to a work camp where he watched Germans kill anyone who couldn't keep up. He was barely fed or clothed. Yet, he had these extraordinary conversations with his wife to sustain him regardless of his circumstance. Why wouldn't we want that for ourselves? Even in the midst of difficult and trying circumstances, you are still the author of your life and your attitude.

Choose well. Make your life the best.

ACKNOWLEDGMENTS

As my book describes several times, life is a team sport and I received the greatest gift in the world when I met Claudia Galvin almost thirty-eight years ago, and we formed a great team that only gets better day after day. Claudia, thank you for always being my rock and fortress; for believing in me when I did not; for loving me when it was hard; and for always being there through the great times and challenging times in our lives. This book could not have been written without you. More importantly, while I know it is not your responsibility to make me happy, being married to you has brought me more joy and happiness than I could have ever imagined.

I am blessed to have had incredibly loving and supportive parents, Don and Pat Hiebert, who, like my older brother Dee, believed in and always encouraged me to be my best self. I especially appreciated my mom's great encouragement to love and embrace my music and artistic self, and so when I find joy in playing piano, guitar, singing, or performing, I think of my mom's enduring love and encouragement. My father was a Green Beret and very charismatic leader who had a distinguished career, retiring from the US Army after thirty-three years of service. It is no surprise that all of his children became leaders who very much subscribed to his values, standards, and understanding that leadership brings with it immense responsibilities to make sure those you are entrusted to lead are more healthy, happy, capable, fulfilled, and successful because of your leadership.

When I married Claudia, as part of the deal I received two other parents that have immensely blessed and inspired my life. My father-in-law, Joseph Galvin, was one of a kind. Having served in WWII in the US Navy Submarine service, Joe went on to a distinguished career, rising to the rank of deputy chief of the New York City Fire Department. Regrettably, like my father, Joe's life was taken by cancer when he had so much more to give the world. Joe was a man of responsible action and I was lucky enough to marry his daughter, who is so much like him. Claudia's mom, Doris, is still going strong at ninety and I am grateful for her great generosity. Over the course of the thirty-eight years we have known each other, she has always treated me with the greatest of kindness.

In addition to my remarkable older brother, I have been enormously blessed to have two other brothers and two sisters, who all are truly amazing as are their marriage partners: Theresa and Paul Horne, Tom and Kate Hiebert, Tim and Lori Hiebert, and Julie and Scott Hodsden. What is amazing is just how disciplined and intentional they all are in living remarkable, joyful, and happy lives. All with the exception of Lori (who was an Air Force brat) have served successfully in the United States Army. All are in the process of raising nineteen wonderful and exceptional children. To all of them: You have provided me unconditional support and affirmation through the years, and your lives truly reflect what this book is all about. I am so proud of every one of you. You all make me a better man, father, and husband. I am grateful for each of you.

When Claudia and I decided we wanted to have children, we didn't realize the crazy and wild journey raising children would be. Emily, Erik, Katie, and Molly: You have made my life incredibly rich and wonderful. During your younger years when I was going through my own internal struggles, I know I was not the best father. Thankfully, your memories are not all that great and I am incredibly grateful that you continue to love, affirm, and support me in such extraordinary ways. I could not have written this book if I did not have your ongoing unconditional support while, when necessary, challenging me as well. My greatest wish for you and your wonderful life partners who are now an integral part of our family, Jerome, Brad and Felicity, is that you each appreciate that happiness and joy is an inside job and that you have everything you need to have the most remarkable and fulfilling lives possible.

I cannot leave out my grandchildren, Judah and Estelle, who have brought me such unexpected joy. Your arrival into the world gave me even more motivation to live long and well, and I hope to be very active in your lives for a long, long time.

Several years ago, I was reflecting on all of the people in my life beyond my family who have inspired, mentored, guided, and helped me be a better man, and I couldn't believe the number of extraordinary friends who have graced my life. Thank you for your amazing friendship; my life has been blessed beyond measure. You also continue to teach me so much about living life with grace, joy, and love. As my book hopefully shows, perhaps the greatest habit we can build into our lives is the habit of building and maintaining strong friendships, and my life is indeed rich.

I have been truly blessed as well over the years by my colleagues who I have worked with at leadership*Forward*, especially, Paul Litten, Rebecca Henson, Michelle Ruiz, and Janet Drey. All of you have helped our company do exceptional work in the pursuit of helping leaders be the best for those they serve and lead. You have made me a much better colleague and human being. Thank you for helping me achieve my dreams.

As this book shares many client stories, I have deliberately changed the names of many of them to protect their confidentiality, while also making sure that they were comfortable with the stories I did share. Ever since I started leadership*Forward* and have coached, taught, mentored, and developed client leaders for the last sixteen years, my life has been enormously purposeful, positive, productive, and profound. And at the heart of that work have been the incredible clients I have had the privilege to serve and support. I find just as Zig Ziglar said many years ago, "You can get everything in life you want if you will just help enough other people get what they want," and in my efforts to help my clients be even more remarkable in their lives as leaders, spouses, parents, and friends, I have benefitted deeply.

Throughout my military, academic, corporate, and consulting careers, I have been greatly blessed by some amazing bosses and leaders who were always trying to strike the right balance between mission accomplishment and taking great care of the people who had to accomplish the mission. I am also grateful to my many West Point classmates who through our class motto, "Strength as One," have helped me grow and held me accountable to our standards of "duty, honor, country." I am equally grateful to my McKinsey and Harvard Business School friends and colleagues who are extraordinary people who work so hard at making a great difference in the world but also work equally hard at being exceptional parents, spouses, friends, and community leaders.

I am also grateful to everyone on my publishing team who helped me so much. Special thanks to Emily, Scott, and Claire for their patience and persistence in helping me get this across the goal line.

Finally, I want to thank God for the gift of life and all the many blessings that have come into and through my life, mostly undeserved but because of God's grace, greatly appreciated, acknowledged, and received.

ABOUT THE AUTHOR

 **GREG HIEBERT** is a highly sought-after leadership coach and educator who has studied the science of resiliency and positive psychology for more than twenty-five years. A graduate of West Point and the Harvard Business School and a former US Army officer, adjunct faculty member of Yale School of Management, and McKinsey consultant, Greg's eclectic mix of experiences allow him to bring a unique wealth of knowledge and perspective to the science of well-being and success. He founded and runs leadership*Forward*, a leadership-performance firm serving clients throughout the country, and he has personally coached hundreds of professionals and teams in several industries, helping them find fulfillment and significance in their life and work.